COGNITIVE THERAPY WITH COUPLES

Frank M. Dattilio, PhD
Center for Cognitive Therapy
University of Pennsylvania
School of Medicine

Christine A. Padesky, PhD
Center for Cognitive Therapy
Newport Beach, California

Professional Resource Exchange, Inc.
P.O. Box 15560
Sarasota, FL 34277-1560

Printed in the United States of America

Paperbound Edition ISBN: 0-943158-49-4
Library of Congress Catalog Card Number: 90-52991

The copy editor for this book was Patricia Hammond, the manag-
ing editor was Debbie Fink, the production assistant was Laurie
Girsch, and the cover designer was Bill Tabler.

FOREWORD

Over the past 25 years, Cognitive Therapy has been applied across an ever-widening spectrum of emotional and behavioral disorders. Its widespread use has been documented and researched in many areas of treatment, including depression, anxiety, substance abuse, eating disorders, and, most recently, personality disorders. An area that is virtually in its infancy, however, is the application of Cognitive Therapy to distressed couples.

In my recent book, *Love Is Never Enough* (Beck, 1988), I delineated the theoretical and practical aspects of cognitive therapy with couples for the general public. Although this has served as a guide for the lay person, as well as for professionals interested in implementing the approach, there has been a need for a more specific outline for therapists wanting to apply the techniques and principles to specific case situations.

I am pleased that Drs. Dattilio and Padesky have decided to undertake the task of preparing this much-needed book. In their preparation, the authors have drawn from the professional research literature and their own clinical experiences in treating distressed couples. In addition, much of the groundwork pioneered by the staff at the Center for Cognitive Therapy, University of Pennsylvania, has also been incorporated in this text.

These two authors bring a wealth of experience to their presentation. Frank Dattilio was a Fellow at our Center for Cognitive Therapy at the University of Pennsylvania and is now a faculty member in Psychiatry (Psychology). He and I have had many discussions on Cognitive Therapy in general as well as with couples. Thanks to his vast experience in treating couples, Dr. Dattilio was able to provide me with helpful case material for my own book and assist me in co-presenting many national workshops and seminars on cognitive therapy with individuals and couples.

Christine Padesky and I have been a teaching team for the past 7 years, presenting over 20 workshops (including cognitive therapy of couples' problems) together throughout the United States and Europe. She is an innovative teacher and clinician with a fresh ear for illustrative case material. Her extensive experience teaching and supervising novices as well as advanced cognitive therapists gives her a rare understanding of the necessary learning points on the road to becoming a cognitive therapist.

Both authors' extensive experience as teachers of cognitive therapy is evident in this book which has a number of case examples illustrating the nuances of the therapy. The inclusion of a full-length case vignette in Chapter 7 provides a first-hand example of the model in action. This case was drawn from a clinical setting and provides a good example of the type of case likely to be encountered by professionals in the field.

This book contains a concise overview of Cognitive Therapy for couples, with detailed descriptions of assessment and therapy procedures. In addition to providing a clear outline of the structure and course of therapy, Dattilio and Padesky provide excellent strategies for identifying and changing beliefs that often interfere with the therapeutic process.

Cognitive Therapy With Couples is an excellent resource for mental health professionals of all therapeutic modalities working with couples in distress. Its clear and concise style makes it accessible to all therapists interested in learning to apply the cognitive model to couples therapy.

Aaron T. Beck, MD
Professor of Psychiatry
University of Pennsylvania
School of Medicine
Philadelphia, Pennsylvania

ABOUT THE AUTHORS

Frank M. Dattilio, PhD, received his doctorate in Psychological Studies from Temple University and completed a clinical post-doctoral fellowship through the Center for Cognitive Therapy at the University of Pennsylvania School of Medicine. He is a licensed psychologist and is listed in the National Register of Health Service Providers in Psychology. A Clinical Member and Approved Supervisor of the American Association of Marriage and Family Therapy, he is also an Adjunct Assistant Professor of Education at Lehigh University, as well as Clinical Associate in Psychiatry (Psychology) at the Center for Cognitive Therapy, University of Pennsylvania. His areas of specialization include individual, marital, and family therapy, and he has authored and co-authored numerous professional articles and chapters on the treatment of behavior disorders, anxiety, and marital discord. Dr. Dattilio has lectured in both the U.S. and Europe and is co-editor with Arthur Freeman, EdD, of *A Casebook in Cognitive-Behavior Therapy* to be released through Plenum Press in 1991.

Christine A. Padesky, PhD, received her doctorate in clinical psychology from UCLA and is Founder and Director of the Center for Cognitive Therapy, Newport Beach, California. She is a licensed psychologist and listed in the National Register of Health Service Providers in Psychology. She is also an Assistant Clinical Professor in the Department of Psychiatry and Human Behavior at the University of California, Irvine. Dr. Padesky has been cited as one of the leading Cognitive Therapy instructors in both the United States and abroad. In addition to being founding editor of the *International Cognitive Therapy Newsletter*, she has written articles and book chapters on depression, anxiety disorders, personality disorders, and cognitive therapy with women. Dr. Padesky is one of the co-authors with Aaron T. Beck, MD, of *Cognitive Therapy of Personality Disorders* (Guilford, 1990).

ACKNOWLEDGEMENTS

Both authors wish to thank all the couples who have so courageously entered therapy to try to understand and change the most important and sometimes most risky part of their lives: their relationships. Each couple teaches their therapist something, especially in such an evolving field as Cognitive Therapy. We also each have our own mentors and associates who have made a difference in our development as therapists and writers.

*　　　*　　　*

First, I would like to thank my teacher and mentor, Aaron T. Beck, for his inexhaustible guidance and encouragement with this project. His support has been the impetus for my optimism during the difficult periods with this process. I also owe much to the publisher, Larry Ritt, who has always remained patient and encouraging throughout the entire production process. Many thanks to my colleagues for their helpful comments on the rough drafts - Francis Gaal, Ruth Greenberg, Shelly Milestone, and Conrad Weiser. In addition, much gratitude is owed to all of my colleagues at the Center for Cognitive Therapy in Philadelphia for their many enlightening suggestions. To our typists: many thanks to Lisa Golba and Deborah Singleton for their expert typing and transcription skills, and Carol Stillman for her professional editorial comments and direction.

Lastly, I thank my wife and children for their love and support during my many absences while preparing this manuscript.

—Frank Dattilio

I would like to thank Aaron T. Beck for his guidance and friendship over the past 12 years. His generosity with ideas and opportunities has helped shape my career. In addition to being appreciative of his well-recognized talents as a theoretician, writer, and researcher, I have always been impressed by the example he sets as a caring and nonjudgmental therapist. Thanks for encouraging me to write more.

Teaching Cognitive Therapy over the past 10 years has been a rich learning experience for me. I want to acknowledge the past post-doctoral fellows at our Center, especially Craig Wiese, who treated many couples of many different cultural backgrounds. Also, thanks go to the many experienced therapists attending supervision groups and intensive teaching programs at our Center who asked insightful questions that deepened my understanding of Cognitive Therapy.

James Shenk and Gail Simpson read drafts of this book and made helpful comments based on their own experiences using Cognitive Therapy with couples. They also helped keep the Center for Cognitive Therapy in Newport Beach running smoothly all the days I stayed home to write. Donald Meichenbaum read an earlier draft of the book and made many excellent suggestions for improvement. My thinking on Cognitive Therapy with couples was helped additionally by workshops and conversations with Janis Abrahms, Norman Epstein, Jean Fromm, and Doris De-Hardt.

Finally, conversations about Cognitive Therapy with Kathleen Mooney over the past 8 years have helped me clarify my understanding of the cognitive model and specify more clearly what I do in therapy. Her creative clinical abilities, sharp editorial skills, and critical analyses have helped me immeasurably in my therapy, writing, teaching, and relationships.

—Christine Padesky

PREFACE

Professionals who treat dysfunctional couples are often reminded of how painstaking psychotherapy can be. This is particularly true for those who treat couples who are in distress or at a volatile period in their lives. Between 1960 and 1974, the divorce rate climbed steadily to a record-breaking figure of 1 million divorces per year. This figure has remained fairly consistent until its recent decline (J. Kelly, 1988). Partly in response to this staggering divorce rate, there has been a resurgence of efforts toward strengthening deteriorating marriages in attempts to maintain the nuclear family and avoid the perils of divorce (Dattilio, 1989b). Consequently, the literature of the past two decades has placed more emphasis on the development of treatment models for couples, with a focus on application.

This book was written for mental health practitioners who work with couples in conflict or distress. It was designed to orient practitioners to the cognitive model of couples therapy and to provide a guide for implementing its various techniques. The cognitive approach is not limited to the treatment of troubled relationships but may also aid in strengthening and enhancing the harmony already existing in basically good relationships.

Therapists who are eclectic in approach, not espousing any particular modality of treatment, will find that this book provides a complete model for effective interventions with couples. Those practitioners who are committed to a particular mode of treatment can use this book as an adjunctive source of techniques to augment their current therapeutic approach.

The contents include an updated literature review of Cognitive Therapy with Couples, along with an overview of Cognitive Therapy itself. The literature review is in broad strokes; those wishing a more comprehensive and detailed review of the research related to cognitive therapy with couples are referred to the work by Baucom and Epstein (1990). The philosophy and theory of Cognitive Therapy with Couples is discussed in depth in this text, along with the specific methods used for assessing dysfunctional relationships. Treatment techniques are discussed in detail, including cognitive aspects of communication training. Other sections deal with the impact of underlying beliefs derived from couples' families of origin, as well as cultural issues and alternative lifestyles. Additional areas addressed are infidelity, polarization, and treatment of couples with concurrent psychiatric disorders (e.g., personality disorders and depression).

A detailed case study is presented as a means of demonstrating a "hands-on" application of the cognitive model. This study was selected because it represents the type of case that practitioners are likely to encounter when dealing with couples in distress, and because it illustrates the specific steps involved in the cognitive approach to treatment. A list of suggested readings is also offered. Ideally, this book should be used in conjunction with a formal course or workshop on Cognitive Therapy. If not, we recommend that the book be read through entirely and the several sections studied in detail before any of the techniques are applied in treatment. We also recommend that supervision be considered for more complicated cases.

The contents of this book are derived from reports of researchers in Cognitive Therapy, and from our own work as clinicians. (Note: The names of clients and their case details have been changed throughout this book to preserve their anonymity.) Authorship order was determined alphabetically because we each made equal contributions to this book. We designed it to be a practitioner's guide that will serve as a "nuts-and-bolts" resource for those professionals seeking to use Cognitive Therapy with couples.

FMD and CAP

TABLE OF
CONTENTS

COGNITIVE THERAPY
WITH COUPLES

1.
OVERVIEW OF COGNITIVE THERAPY

HISTORICAL DEVELOPMENT

In the past two decades, Cognitive Therapy has been one of the fastest growing, and become one of the most popular, modalities of therapy (Patterson, 1980; Ritter, 1985; Smith, 1982). Actually, more than 20 therapies have been called "cognitive" or "cognitive-behavioral" (Mahoney & Lyddon, 1988). Therefore, it is important to specify what is meant by Cognitive Therapy.

In this book, Cognitive Therapy refers to the theory, therapy, and conceptual models developed by Aaron T. Beck, MD, and his associates (Beck, 1976, 1988; Beck, Emery, & Greenberg, 1985; Beck et al., 1990; Beck, Rush, et al., 1979). Although the therapy is called "cognitive," in fact there is an emphasis on the interaction among five elements: environment (including developmental history and culture), biology, affect, behavior, and cognition (Padesky, 1986).

The term cognitive was used to describe this five-part interactive therapy model because, in the 1960s and early 1970s, most therapies tended to give less attention to the cognitive aspects of a client's problem than to affect, biology, behavior, or developmental history. Because Beck's therapy was among the first to give close attention to the impact of thinking on affect, behavior, biology, and experience of the environment, it was natural at that time to call the therapy "cognitive." Unfortunately, the name of the therapy has led to several misunderstandings.

1

The first misunderstanding is that some writers and therapists think the cognitive model states that thoughts cause feelings or behaviors. This is a myth. Ellis (1962) wrote that thoughts cause feelings as part of the theory of Rational-Emotive Therapy (another "cognitive" therapy developed in the 1960s). In contrast, as an interactive model, Cognitive Therapy states that thoughts, feelings, behaviors, biology, and environment are each capable of influencing the others.

Thoughts are often emphasized in Cognitive Therapy because Beck's research demonstrated that distortions in thoughts often serve to maintain dysfunctional mood states. Also, changes in beliefs can lead to changes in affect and/or behavior. Therefore, thoughts are seen as a key point of intervention in Cognitive Therapy. This does not mean, however, that the cognitive therapist regards thoughts as the necessary cause of psychological distress.

A related misconception about Cognitive Therapy is that the therapy is purely cognitive. In fact, cognitive therapists pay close attention to affect and behavior. The second chapter of the classic text, *Cognitive Therapy of Depression* (Beck, Rush, et al., 1979), is titled "The Role of Emotions in Cognitive Therapy." This chapter discusses the importance of emotion in human experience and the necessity for therapists to empathize with client feelings in cognitive therapy.

More recently, Beck stated that Cognitive Therapy cannot be conducted in the absence of affect. The therapist should be skilled at eliciting affect if the client does not express it spontaneously (Beck & Padesky, 1987). Similarly, cognitive therapists need an understanding of behavior patterns and behavioral methods for change since these also have always been central to Cognitive Therapy.

Because it is often a brief therapy, some critics have charged that Cognitive Therapy focuses only on surface, symptomatic changes. As will be seen in the case vignettes throughout this book, Cognitive Therapy operates at several levels. There is an emphasis on here-and-now problems in clients' lives. The cognitive therapist's goal is to teach clients methods for resolving current problems and sources of distress. To accomplish this, the therapist looks for the core of the problem rather than sticking to surface issues. The case study at the end of the book (see Chapter 7) illustrates this process.

At the cognitive level of change, the therapist works at three levels. The most accessible, "surface" thoughts are referred to as *automatic thoughts.* These are thoughts (ideas, beliefs, images) people have each moment which are situation specific (e.g., "My husband is late. He doesn't care about my feelings" and/or a quick image of her husband laughing with co-workers). At a deeper level are conditional rules and cross-situational beliefs called *underlying assumptions.* These rules help organize our perceptions and are the roots of the automatic thoughts (e.g., "You can't count on men to be there for you"). Finally, at the core are basic beliefs called *schemas* which are inflexible unconditional beliefs (e.g., "I'll always be alone").

These three levels of thought are interconnected; Cognitive Therapy hopes to effect change at all three levels. Because the automatic thoughts are most flexible and testable, the therapist begins with these in the early stages of therapy. The client learns to test these thoughts with automatic thought records, as described in Chapter 4. Once the client can identify and test automatic thoughts with ease, the therapist helps the client identify the underlying assumptions which give rise to frequently occurring automatic thoughts. These assumptions can be tested on paper or, more ideally, through behavioral experiments (e.g., "Ask your husband to be there for you, and see if he follows through when he knows what you want"). Finally, schemas can be tested and changed and are a primary focus of treatment interventions with clients having personality disorders (see Chapter 6).

The process of Cognitive Therapy has been described as "collaborative empiricism" (Beck, Rush, et al., 1979). It is collaborative because the therapist and client work together in partnership to understand and solve the client's problems. Empiricism refers to the process of collecting data to evaluate the evidence for and against current and alternative beliefs.

The theoretical underpinnings of Cognitive Therapy have been shaped by a variety of approaches, including phenomenology, structural theory, and cognitive psychology. According to the phenomenological approach, the individual's view of the self and the personal world are central to the determination of behavior (Adler, 1936; Horney, 1950). Structural theory, on the other hand, emphasizes the concept of hierarchical structuring of cognitive processes with an emphasis on the division into primary and secondary process thinking. Integrating aspects of both theories, cognitive psychology stresses the importance of cognition in information processing and behavioral change.

3

Cognitive Therapy began in the early 1960s as a result of Beck's research on depression (Beck, 1963, 1964, 1967/1972). This work was undertaken in an attempt to validate Freud's theory that depression results from anger turned inward toward the self. In his efforts to substantiate this theory, Beck made clinical observations of depressed patients and examined their dreams and thought content in accordance with the principles of traditional psychoanalysis. Rather than finding retroflected anger in their thoughts and dreams, he observed a negative bias in the cognitive processing of depressed individuals. After conducting a number of clinical studies and investigations, Beck developed the cognitive theory of emotional disorders (Beck, 1976), and then went on to delineate the cognitive model of depression (Beck, Rush, et al., 1979).

Cognitive Therapy drew upon the work of a number of earlier writers. One of the most influential therapists was George A. Kelly (1955), who developed a model of personal constructs and beliefs connected to behavioral change. Kelly defined a construct as an individual's way of construing or interpreting the world. His interest focused on observing how an individual places structure and meaning on these particular constructs. Subsequent to Kelly's work, cognitive theories of emotion, such as those developed by Magda Arnold (1960) and Richard Lazarus (1966) proposed that change in cognition was primary in emotional and behavioral change.

The work of Albert Ellis (1962) in Rational-Emotive Therapy (RET) has provided support to the principles of Cognitive Therapy and impetus to the development of what is now known as Cognitive-Behavioral Therapy. Both Rational-Emotive Therapy and Cognitive Therapy contend that individuals adopt reasoning patterns and possess control over their thoughts and actions. Both approaches view the underlying assumptions that generate these reasoning patterns as targets of intervention in therapy. In both approaches, the therapist works to obtain the specific content of the patients' cognitions and/or beliefs. Patients are taught to identify and report in detail their dysfunctional cognitions, including when they occur and their impact on the patient's feelings.

According to Ellis (1973, 1980), RET therapists work to persuade individuals that the beliefs they have are irrational, and offer to teach them a more adaptive philosophy of living. Beck, on the other hand, proposed that clients could learn to evaluate their own cognitions if the therapist collaborated with clients in testing the validity of their beliefs (Beck, Kovacs, & Weisman, 1979). Emphasis is placed on the collaborative aspect of the approach, on the assumption that people learn to change their thinking more readily if the rationale for change comes from their own insights rather than from the therapist's.

For example, one client may have the belief, "If Susan doesn't approve of everything I do, then she will leave me." Ellis' approach in working with this client would most likely involve *challenging* this belief. The therapist might say, "What makes Susan such a supreme judge? You're acting as if it is awful if she doesn't love everything about you. That's nonsense - no one loves everything about anybody." The Cognitive Therapy approach with this same client would involve *testing* this belief. The therapist might say, "I can see how that belief would frighten you. Let's test it and see if it's true. Has Susan ever not liked something you've done? When that happened, did she leave you? What did she do instead? Was that a totally negative outcome, or did something useful come from that experience?"

In Cognitive Therapy, the collaborative relationship between therapist and client provides a forum in which the client can begin to learn the processes for identifying and testing dysfunctional thoughts. The goal of this therapy is not only to change current dysfunctional beliefs, but also to teach the client methods he or she can use in the future to evaluate other beliefs.

A number of contemporary behaviorists have also had an impact on the growth and development of Cognitive Therapy. The social learning theory of Albert Bandura (1977), which involves the conceptualization of new behavior patterns (observational learning), has contributed to the cognitive model and serves as a guide for action in participant modeling. This theory encouraged and promoted the shift in Behavior Therapy to the cognitive domain. Mahoney's (1974) early work on cognitive control of behavior and Meichenbaum's work (1977) on cognitive behavior modification have also made important theoretical contributions.

Cognitive Therapy gained recognition initially as a mode of treatment for depression (Beck, 1970, 1976). Research has provided empirical support for the model and its effectiveness in cases of unipolar depression (Beck & Rush, 1978). Studies comparing Cognitive Therapy and antidepressant medications have also been conducted (Beck, 1986; Hollon et al., 1985; Murphy et al., 1984). In several outcome comparisons, Cognitive Therapy was shown to be equal in effectiveness to antidepressant

5

medication in treating depression. Still more impressively, the double-blind study of Rush et al. (1977) demonstrated that cognitive psychotherapy was more effective than medication in the alleviation of depression. The research of Kovacs et al. (1981) suggested that Cognitive Therapy has a lower rate of relapse than psychopharmacological treatments, and other studies have supported this finding (Blackburn et al., 1981; Murphy et al., 1984).

As an offshoot to the work on depression, the development of concepts for the treatment of suicidal clients has gained attention (Beck, Schuyler, & Herman, 1974; Freeman & White, 1989). A major finding of the work of Beck and his colleagues was that hopelessness was a key component of suicidal intent and outcome. As a result of his work, Beck generated a number of assessment scales for depression and suicidality, such as the Beck Depression Inventory (Beck et al., 1961), the Scale for Suicide Ideation (Beck, Kovacs, et al., 1979), the Suicide Intent Scale (Beck, Schuyler, et al., 1974), and the Hopelessness Scale (Beck, Weisman, et al., 1974).

Cognitive Therapy has also devoted research and attention to the study of anxiety disorders (Beck & Emery, 1979; Beck, Emery, et al., 1985; Beck, Epstein, et al., 1985; Beck, Laude, & Bohnert, 1974; Dattilio, 1987, 1988, 1990b; Ottaviani & Beck, 1987), personality disorders (Beck et al., 1990; Pretzer & Fleming, 1989), and marital discord (Baucom & Epstein, 1990; Beck, 1988; Dattilio, 1989a, 1989b; Epstein, 1986; Schlesinger & Epstein, 1986), which will be highlighted in more detail in the overview presented in Chapter 2.

PHILOSOPHY AND THEORY

Although Cognitive Therapy is rooted in some of the more traditional systems of therapy, it differs with some of the theories of the psychodynamic, behavioral, and neuropsychiatric modalities. Cognitive Therapy emphasizes that what individuals think and perceive about themselves, their world, and the future is relevant and important and has a direct impact on how they feel and behave. The view of self, world, and future is called the "cognitive triad," first introduced in Beck's cognitive model of depression (Beck, 1976, Beck, Rush, et al., 1979).

In addition to biological and environmental factors, Cognitive Therapy views personality as being shaped by central beliefs or superordinate schemas. Schemas develop early in life as a result of personal experiences and parental and societal influences. They constitute the basis for coding, categorizing, and evaluating experiences during the course of one's life.

Psychological problems are perceived as stemming from commonplace processes such as faulty learning, making incorrect inferences on the basis of inadequate or incorrect information, and not distinguishing adequately between imagination and reality (Kovacs & Beck, 1979). Individuals often formulate rules or standards that are excessively rigid and absolutist, based on erroneous assumptions. Such standards are derived from schemas, or complex patterns of thoughts that determine how experiences will be perceived and conceptualized. These schemas or thought patterns are usually employed even in the absence of environmental data. They may serve as a type of transformation mechanism that shapes the incoming data so as to fit and reinforce preconceived notions (Beck & Emery, 1979). For example, a man who has the schema, "I am doomed to fail," will read a work evaluation as negative even if it is generally positive or neutral.

This distortion of experience is maintained through the operation of characteristic errors in information processing. Beck (1979) proposes that several types of fallacious thinking contribute to the feedback loops that support psychological disorders. For example, systematic errors in reasoning, which are termed "cognitive distortions," are present during psychological distress and include the following: arbitrary inferences, selective personalization, dichotomous thinking, labeling and mislabeling, tunnel vision, biased explanations, and mind reading. These terms are explained in more detail in Chapter 4 under "Identifying Cognitive Distortions and Labeling Them."

One goal of the cognitive therapeutic process is to aid clients in unraveling their cognitive distortions and to collaboratively develop more balanced ways of evaluating their experiences. There are a host of therapeutic techniques designed to identify such errors in reasoning and to test them against reality. Learning these methods enables the individual to correct the distortions and dysfunctional beliefs (schemas) that give rise to these cognitions. In essence, then, the individual learns to correct faulty thinking that he or she had believed to be infallible. This is accomplished by identifying predictions based on dysfunctional beliefs, then testing them by gathering additional evidence. The therapist helps the client compare the validity of dysfunctional beliefs with alternative explanations. The focus is on collabora-

7

tively encouraging the individual to adopt these alternative responses as part of his or her overall thinking style, hence creating a new way of viewing life events. The application of these techniques to relationships is described in detail in Chapter 2.

2.
COGNITIVE THERAPY
WITH COUPLES

BRIEF HISTORY AND OVERVIEW

As compared with other approaches to couples therapy, Cognitive Therapy with Couples is still in its infancy. The cognitive approach to couples therapy stems directly from the application of behavioral theory to marital therapy. Its effectiveness has sparked further investigation into its application. Since the development of Behavioral Marital therapy, there have been a number of innovative changes. The initial introduction of behavioral treatment approaches placed emphasis on social exchange theory and contingency contracting with couples (Bandura, 1977; Jacobson & Margolin, 1979; Liberman, 1970; Liberman, Wheeler, & Sanders, 1976; Patterson & Hops, 1972; Stuart, 1969, 1976).

Stuart's theory is one of the more comprehensive and popular among the behavioral approaches. Stuart contends that the most effective way to initiate relationship change is to increase the rate at which the partners exchange positive behaviors. He uses a technique called "caring days," which aids the partners in achieving their treatment goals. Stuart's approach involves an eight-step program with such features as behavioral contracting and communication training. Although behavioral techniques can be effective, they sometimes fail to bring about attitudinal or cognitive changes in the individuals (Patterson, 1986). Therefore, a limitation of Behavior Marital Therapy is that it places little emphasis on individuals' thinking styles about themselves and their partners. Cognitive Therapy differs from the behavior-

9

al approach in that it places the predominant emphasis on the thought processes and belief systems of the partners while still recognizing the need for behavioral change.

The addition of a cognitive component to behavioral couples therapy developed as a result of early studies such as the one conducted by Margolin and Weiss (1978) which compared Behavioral Marital Therapy with a treatment supplementing Behavioral Marital Therapy with cognitive restructuring techniques. The authors found that treatment including cognitive restructuring components was significantly more effective than Behavioral Marital Therapy alone on several outcome measures. During the subsequent decade of research, cognitive techniques became a major focus in the couples therapy literature (Baucom, 1981; Baucom & Epstein, 1990; Beck, 1988; Dattilio, 1989a, 1990a; Doherty, 1981; Fincham & O'Leary, 1983; Holtzworth-Munroe & Jacobson, 1985; Jacobson, 1983, 1984; Jacobson et al., 1985; Margolin, 1983; Margolin, Christensen, & Weiss, 1975; Revenstorf, 1984; Schindler & Vollmer, 1984; Weiss, 1980, 1984). Since the intent of this book is to focus on clinical intervention, the interested reader is referred to Baucom and Epstein (1990) for a comprehensive review of research findings related to cognition, affect, and behavior in cognitive therapy with couples.

Ellis (1977) was among the first to report a predominantly cognitive approach with couples. Building on his work in Rational-Emotive Therapy in the 1960s, Ellis proposed that marital dysfunction occurs when spouses maintain unrealistic expectations about marriage and make extreme negative evaluations when they are not satisfied. He contends that disturbed feelings and behaviors in relationships are not caused merely by one's mate's wrongdoing or other adverse events, but by the views that partners take of each other's actions and life's rough breaks (Ellis et al., 1989). Rational-emotive theory posits that thinking, feeling, and acting are quite interactional and that each of these processes continually influences and affects the other two. Ellis states that disturbed marriages result when one or both spouses hold irrational beliefs - irrational being defined as highly exaggerated, inappropriately rigid, illogical, and absolutist. As a result of this irrational thinking, unrealistic and demanding expectations develop which produce disappointment and frustration when they are perceived as being violated. These responses, in turn, give rise to negative emotions which contribute to a vicious cycle of disturbance.

Rational-Emotive Therapy challenges the validity of spouses' irrational beliefs and teaches spouses how to replace their faulty thinking with more realistic thoughts about themselves and their partners.

Cognitive Therapy with Couples differs from Rational-Emotive Therapy by combining many of the insights from the psychodynamic therapies, along with many of the strategies introduced by Behavior Therapy. The conventional approaches are combined within a cognitive framework with an emphasis on specific concepts involving general thinking styles, underlying beliefs about the relationship, and the nature of current interactions between the partners.

Cognitive Therapy with Couples and Rational-Emotive Therapy share the basic goal of testing the evidence that supports or refutes partners' beliefs about themselves and their relationships. In the cognitive approach to couples therapy, collaboration among therapist and partners is emphasized. This collaboration is based on the philosophy that such a conjoint effort minimizes client resistance and introduces coping skills that couples can apply independent of the therapeutic setting. Much time is dedicated to testing the reality of the couple's beliefs about the nature of intimacy in the relationship. Rational-Emotive Therapy, on the other hand, promotes a change of partners' evaluative beliefs about perceived events in a more directive fashion.

With the cognitive movement in psychotherapy, it appeared only logical that cognitions that were held by couples about each other needed to be an integral part of the change process. It is believed that behavior change alone is insufficient to effect permanent resolution of the type of intense dysfunctional interactions often experienced by couples on a day-to-day basis. It is, therefore, the goal of Cognitive Therapy with Couples to address the belief structures of each partner in order to promote restructuring toward a more productive relationship.

There are three major cognitive facets in Cognitive Therapy with Couples: (a) modification of unrealistic expectations in the relationship, (b) correction of faulty attributions in relationship interactions, and (c) the use of self-instructional procedures to decrease destructive interaction. One of the primary concerns of the cognitive therapist in couples therapy is identifying the partners' schemas or beliefs about relationships in general and, more specifically, their thoughts about their own relationship (Beck, 1988; Epstein, 1986).

Basic beliefs about relationships and the nature of couple interaction are often learned early in life from primary sources such as parents, local cultural mores, the media, and early dating experiences. These schemas, or dysfunctional beliefs about relationships, are often not articulated clearly in an individual's mind but may exist as vague concepts of what should be (Beck, 1988). These beliefs can, however, be derived from the logic and themes of one's automatic thoughts.

The cognitive therapist working with couples must focus equally on each partner's expectations about the nature of an intimate relationship. In addition, the distortions in evaluations of experience derived from those expectations are critically important. For example, a husband who believes his wife is interested in every man she glances at might therefore expect her to refrain from looking at any other individual, male or female.

With respect to automatic thoughts, the cognitive therapist assumes that unrealistic expectations about relationships can erode satisfaction and elicit dysfunctional responses. For example, many couples enter a relationship with the belief that love spontaneously occurs between two people and exists that way forever without further effort. As a result, couples may experience a decrease in satisfaction once they realize that hard work is necessary to maintain their relationship. This expectation may also lead to inaccurate appraisals such as "We probably were not right for each other from the start." Epstein and Eidelson (1981) found that adherence to unrealistic beliefs concerning the nature of intimate relationships was predictive of distress level in relationships. Therefore, cognitive content is extremely important in accounting for dysfunctional responses to relationship conflicts.

Cognitive distortions may be evident in the automatic thoughts that couples report and may be uncovered by means of systematic or Socratic questioning regarding the meaning that a partner attaches to a specific event. Spouses' automatic thoughts about their interactions with one another commonly include inferences about the causes of pleasant and unpleasant events that occur between them.

In his book, *Love Is Never Enough*, Beck (1988) has described several systematic distortions in information processing that occur frequently in automatic thoughts concerning relationships. For example, the thought, "He always puts me down," is more likely to be an instance of generalization than an accurate accounting of a spouse's invariant behavior. As another example, in the absence of concrete evidence, the thought, "She thinks I am an idiot," would be an arbitrary inference.

Cognitive Therapy with Couples focuses on the cognitions that are identified as components of relationship discord and as contributing to each partner's subjective dissatisfaction with the relationship (Schlesinger & Epstein, 1986). This approach moves to the core of relationship difficulty by focusing on hidden as well as obvious here-and-now problems, rather than by dwelling on early childhood traumas. A wife, for example, may show explosive rage toward her husband. If he is not provoking such intense anger, she may find that her rage has other meanings. One woman discovered that her rage was preceded by a feeling of helplessness. In fact, she had an image of herself as a young child screaming to be heard by her mother as she was locked in a car. Once the therapy helped her identify this underlying fear that she would not be heard unless she screamed, she was able to begin to explore alternative methods of expressing her feelings to her husband.

There are several major focal areas in the cognitive model that are essential when addressing the issue of change in relationships. These are outlined in detail below.

BELIEFS ABOUT THE RELATIONSHIP

Basic beliefs are the foundation for individuals' automatic thoughts and actions in any relationship. In order to understand these thoughts and actions, the therapist must work to uncover the basic belief system and develop a clear understanding of how each spouse views their relationship and his or her role in relationships in general. As in the example of the wife who responded with destructive rage, the emphasis is placed on hidden, as well as obvious, here-and-now problems, as opposed to dwelling on early childhood traumas. Beneath her anger was a sense of vulnerability and helplessness. By uncovering this basic schema, the therapist was able to help her define ways in which she could be heard and share some control of her relationship without verbally attacking her husband. By discovering this underlying issue, she was further able to see that she viewed many relationships as manipulative and controlling even when they were not. Her view of herself as helpless and childlike had prevented her from being assertive with her own needs until she was furious. By learning to assert her needs more consistently and to express her anger in ways that her husband would hear, she was able to re-

13

duce not only her anger, but feel more empowered in the relationship.

Much of the cognitive approach involves ferreting out couples' basic beliefs and then collaboratively redefining key principles and restructuring the belief system. The amount of restructuring required varies, but it is recommended the restructuring process be done with each person in the presence of the mate. By witnessing the testing and restructuring of beliefs, each partner is better able to provide support later in the process of treatment. This technique is illustrated in the case study presented in Chapter 7. Basic beliefs about the relationship are thus important in attempting to incur change with couples. Uncovering the basic belief system allows the therapist to teach individuals the first step in altering their view of the relationship.

ALTERNATIVE VERSUS DISTORTED BELIEFS

When working with couples, there is often disagreement over whether thoughts are balanced or distorted. In Cognitive Therapy, balanced beliefs are designated as beliefs that have substantiating or supportive evidence. These are beliefs that are not convoluted by an individual's biases or misperceptions. Distorted beliefs, on the other hand, are beliefs which are based on misinformation or faulty thinking and are usually rooted in circumstantial evidence. An example of a common distorted belief is the statement, "All men are alike." In the context of a relationship, this view carries negative connotations and represents a class of cognitive distortion called generalization. If maintained under all circumstances, such a belief represents distorted thinking. Another example might be a husband who believes, "I must help my wife resolve every one of her dilemmas in order to be a good husband." This again becomes a distorted belief when adhered to steadfastly.

The alternative version of such statements usually includes more explanations with conditions attached. For example, for the belief, "All men are alike," the more balanced view might be, "All men are alike in many ways, yet each is also unique." In the example of the statement, "I must help my wife resolve every one of her dilemmas in order to be a good husband," a more balanced/alternative statement might be, "It's important that I offer assistance to my wife when I can or be there for her when she needs me."

Distorted beliefs are often the basis of much dissension in relationships and need to be addressed quite specifically in order to introduce change in the relationship. They usually develop as a result of faulty thought patterns that become a part of the individual's common thought processes. Regardless of how they developed, the therapist's role is to help weigh the existing evidence and test predictions made on the basis of the belief in order to assess its reasonableness. Chapter 4 explains the procedure in greater detail.

UNREALISTIC EXPECTATIONS

The expectations that each person brings to the relationship create important dynamics in each union and have been a focus for most cognitive therapists treating distressed couples (Epstein, 1982; Jacobson & Margolin, 1979).

With almost every relationship, individuals hold some anticipation with regard to the multitude of needs their partner will fulfill for them. Very often, these expectations or anticipations lead to distortions and are transformed into unrealistic demands. It may take awhile for some of these expectations to assert themselves in the relationship, which would account for why they become an issue only after a period of time in many relationships, as opposed to during the courtship period. Beck (1988) and Ellis et al. (1989) contend that unrealistic or demanding expectations inevitably produce disappointment and frustration which is often associated with negative interactions (e.g., hostility, badgering, etc.). A common example of this pattern occurs in the couple who enter a relationship with the expectation that love spontaneously occurs between two people and exists that way forever with virtually little or no further effort on either partner's part. Such a couple experience deep disappointment and hurt when problems arise and may even erroneously conclude that their difficulties signal that the relationship was never really a good one. In this example, the unrealistic expectation is held by both spouses simultaneously, but oftentimes, unrealistic expectations are held by one person in direct conflict with the other's viewpoint.

For example, one man who came from an environment where the father was the sole breadwinner expected his wife to be content in remaining home and not working outside the home. However, his wife was reared to believe that partners have equal rights, and this created a conflict over her wish to seek employment. Such expectations emanate from early conceptualizations about relationships, spousal roles, and individual needs. These conceptualizations are derived from primary sources such as parents, the media, and early dating experiences. They are usually blended with each partner's personal ideas of how he or she would like the relationship to be.

In addressing unrealistic expectations, the therapist must again refer to the root of both partners' belief systems. The therapist taps into their cognitive schemas and teaches them first to identify erroneous beliefs via comparisons and then to test these beliefs against alternative evidence. This is usually done one step at a time. It is important to go slowly and not to "upset the applecart" too quickly. It is essential to remember that individuals have become dependent on these underlying belief structures, and removing them too quickly may create resistance on either partner's part.

CAUSAL ATTRIBUTIONS AND MISATTRIBUTIONS

Causal attribution is a formal term for "laying blame" in the relationship. It is not uncommon for spouses to arrive for therapy in a vicious blaming cycle which is propelled by anger, resentment, and the refusal of both to accept responsibility for the dysfunction in the relationship. Consequently, there exists an externalization of blame and a misattribution of the problem to the actions of the partner. If they are both stubborn individuals, then the couple remain in a deadlock in which they inadvertently attempt to place the therapist in the uncomfortable position of determining who is to blame.

Some authors believe (Abrahms, 1982) that conflict resolution or communication training is impossible unless both partners are willing to collaborate. The term "collaborative set" was coined by Jacobson and Margolin (1979) to indicate the need for both partners to behave in a manner that suggests that they view their conflicts as mutual and that the conflicts are likely to be resolved only by working conjointly to solve them. Even if this stance is adopted overtly, couples may individually harbor thoughts about the attribution of blame which will later infiltrate the relationship. Therefore, another important step in the restructuring process involves helping both partners to accept responsibility for the distress in the relationship. This requires discussions and evaluation of the causal attributions each partner has made for the relationship problems.

These areas - beliefs about the relationship, alternative versus distorted beliefs, unrealistic expectations, and causal attributions and misattributions - are all targeted in the Cognitive Therapy model. The following chapters concern the assessment and interventions of the approach, addressing the process of change in these basic areas of marital dysfunction in more detail.

3.
ASSESSMENT

OVERVIEW

There are many methods for conducting the clinical interview, and clinicians choose a method and style to suit their unique personalities. Regardless of personal style, however, certain structure and content are necessary for good clinical assessment, just as a tennis player adds his or her special touch to delivery of the ball, yet follows certain rules and standards of good tennis. In the cognitive approach, there are three essential steps in the initial assessment phase: conjoint interviews, the administration of assessment inventories and questionnaires, and individual interviews. This is the standard procedure used with the cognitive approach unless a crisis is at hand. Depending on the nature of the crisis, the standard sequence may be interrupted to accommodate the circumstances (see Chapter 6).

As with most couples therapy approaches, the initial session will typically be a conjoint interview. A conjoint interview gives the therapist an initial impression of how the couples interact and an opportunity to "learn their dance" as the system theorists have coined it. This initial impression is extremely important because it provides the interviewing therapist with a flavor of the problems at hand and reveals the type of guardedness the couple may be prone to use when interacting publicly. It also provides insight for the therapist as to the couple's suitability for therapy.

Ideally, the treating therapist will be the same individual who conducts the intake. Many clinics or community outpatient mental health centers have a particular individual designated to conduct intakes only. If at all possible, the intake should be done by the treating therapist in order for him or her to become familiar with the case and begin to establish an effective rapport. At this time, the couple should also be informed that the first few sessions will involve problem definition and relationship assessment and that they should not expect immediate change until therapy progresses. This may help reduce unrealistic expectations that one or both spouses bring to treatment - or at least bring these expectations into the open.

CONJOINT INTERVIEWS

The initial interview is conjoint with a focus on obtaining background information regarding how and under what circumstances the couple met, whether or not they live together, the number of years living together or married, whether or not they were previously married or in long-term relationships, the number and ages of children from this and previous relationships, and a brief history of the presenting problems. A specific form has been developed by the Center for Cognitive Therapy in Philadelphia for the purpose of intake (see "Clinician's Intake Evaluation for Couples," pp. 33-38). Additional information may be gathered in subsequent sessions or as the therapy proceeds.

Often, couples will withhold information, either knowingly or unknowingly, that might be vital to understanding the dynamics of the relationship. For a multitude of reasons, this information often will surface later during the treatment process. It can then be incorporated into the conceptualization of the relationship. Therefore, the information-gathering process should not be shut off after the first three sessions. The therapist might also ask the couple, "Is there anything else that I should know to help me understand your relationship problems?" The background is essential and should be given adequate attention. It allows the therapist to formulate a preliminary conceptualization of how both spouses see their relationship and view the course of their conflict.

WRITTEN INVENTORIES
AND QUESTIONNAIRES

Because the intake process is limited by time, several written surveys and questionnaires can be used that have been designed to assess and change attitudes and beliefs about the relationship. They are oriented specifically toward identifying dysfunctional thoughts, problems in communication, and pleasing as well as displeasing behaviors. These instruments are also one method for allowing couples to pinpoint the specific areas of their conflict and to mention additional information that they may have been reluctant or embarrassed to mention during the conjoint interview.

The specific inventories popularly used by cognitive therapists include the following:

Marital Attitude Questionnaire-Revised: This was derived from the Marital Attitude Questionnaire (Pretzer, Fleming, & Epstein, 1983). This questionnaire contains 74 statements which are designed to determine how each spouse views the difficulties in the relationship. It consists of such statements as "When we aren't getting along, I wonder if my partner loves me" and "Stress from working influences how we get along." The statements are rated on a 5-point Likert scale with 1 meaning "strongly agree" and 5 meaning "strongly disagree." The scores are then tallied to obtain an overall score.

Dyadic Adjustment Scale (DAS; Spanier, 1976): This is a self-report inventory of adjustment in relationships (couples). Thirteen consensus items in the areas of household tasks, finances, recreation, friends, religion, decision-making, and so on, are measured with regard to the degree that the spouse reports agreement or disagreement. This instrument assesses global marital distress and yields an overall score on the interrelated aspects of relationship adjustment.

Marital Happiness Scale (MHS; Azrin, Naster, & Jones, 1973): The degree of happiness is assessed across 11 domains (e.g., child-rearing, financial, communication, etc.). Spouses rate on a 10-point scale from "completely unhappy" to "completely happy" how they view each domain in the relationship. This inventory provides a rather quick overview of the couples' distress.

Marital Satisfaction Inventory (MSI; Snyder, 1981): This is a dichotomous forced-choice (true/false) inventory constituted of 280 items embedded in nine domain areas such as: child-rearing, finances, sexual problems, communication, family history, and so

21

on. A global distress scale is also included to provide the clinician with an overall rating of distress. The couples' scores can then be plotted out on a profile sheet together in order to compare their perceptions of the difficulties in the relationship with each other.

There are also a number of other inventories that have not been empirically validated, but which are very helpful in pinpointing problem areas with couples:

Beliefs About Change Questionnaire (Beck, 1988): This is an open-ended questionnaire in checklist format. It requests the reader to check statements which reflect a particular belief held, for example: "My partner is incapable of change" and "My marriage is dead." The questionnaire is categorized under four headings: Defeatist Beliefs, Self-Justifying Beliefs, Reciprocity Arguments, and Problem Is My Partner. No overall score is obtained.

Problems in the Partnership (Beck, 1988): This is a list of 42 issues commonly found among couples. The reader is asked to rate such statements as "We disagree" or "I give in" on a scale from 0 (does not apply) to 4 (all of the time). The reader is also asked to indicate whether or not these are perceived as problems in the relationship. The statements are divided into four areas: Making Decisions, Finances, Sex Relations, and Recreation and Leisure Activities.

Expressions of Love (Beck, 1988): This checklist was designed as a way for couples to identify the manner in which they show each other affection and caring. The individual is instructed to determine how frequently he or she can answer either yes or no to such questions as: "Do you miss your partner when you are apart?" or "Are you able to determine and respect your partner's sensitive areas?" The individual is requested to rate the questions on a Likert scale from 0 (never) to 5 (always). The questionnaire is divided into 12 areas with three questions in each area: Feelings of Warmth, Expressions of Affection, Caring, Acceptance and Tolerance, Empathy and Sensitivity, Understanding, Companionship, Intimacy, Friendliness, Pleasing, Support, and Closeness. There are no absolute scores for rating the questionnaire.

Problems in the Style of Communication (Beck, 1988): This checklist is a measure of styles of talking and listening that can hinder the exchange of ideas and information. Individuals are asked to rate the behaviors that their partner uses with them on a Likert scale from 0 (does not apply) to 4 (all of the time). In another column they are requested to rate how much the problems bother them, from 0 (not at all) to 3 (a great deal). This is based on 15 statements such as "Talks too much" or "Withdraws when upset." There is no absolute score.

Inventories and questionnaires may serve several purposes. First, they provide an initial exercise for couples to perform, which may indicate a great deal to the therapist, particularly if the couples procrastinate in completing them. They may also serve as an indirect means of ventilation for angry or resentful spouses. Third, they serve as a standard measure of dysfunction for both the couple and therapist and may be administered later at varying intervals throughout the course of treatment. This will aid the therapist in monitoring treatment progress.

Although it is not always the normal procedure, the therapist may also wish to conduct a further clinical assessment, particularly if he or she suspects more significant psychopathology. Such instruments as the Structured Clinical Interview for *DSM-III-R* (SCID) (Spitzer, Williams, & Gibbon, 1987) or the Minnesota Multiphasic Personality Inventory-2 (MMPI-2; Butcher et al., 1989) may serve as diagnostic aids in planning the treatment course. This will likewise rule out any need for additional treatments (e.g., psychiatric, etc.). See Chapter 6 for a more detailed discussion of this.

INDIVIDUAL INTERVIEWS

Subsequent to the initial conjoint interview, an individual interview is conducted with each partner. This serves a number of purposes. It provides the therapist with the opportunity to interact with each person when the partner is not present. If, for example, a man is intimidated by his wife's presence, it may be easier to observe this by noticing the difference when he is interviewed alone. This may also hold true with the expression of his thoughts about the relationship. Initially, one partner may be reluctant to say exactly how he or she feels in front of the other for fear of hurting the other or causing an angry reaction. The areas covered in the individual session should include those areas not discussed in the conjoint session, such as any sexual or physical abuse experienced as a child or adult; incidents of rape; details about past relationships or extramarital affairs; successes or failures; issues regarding family of origin; any violence in the current relationship; and any specific information that the client prefers be kept confidential, at least for the time being.

With regard to the content, the focus should be on developing a conceptualization of how the individual views the problems in the relationship. Emphasis is placed on specific automatic thoughts and beliefs about himself or herself and the changes needing to occur in the relationship. This is highlighted in more detail later in this chapter.

At this point the therapist needs to make some determination about the course of treatment. Much of this will depend on the information and perspective the therapist gathers on each individual. For example, should one partner confide that he or she is involved in an extramarital affair, this will no doubt have a significant impact on the course of treatment. Another common circumstance is one spouse informing the therapist that he or she "wants out" of the relationship and that the therapy is simply a means of justifying that "last ditch efforts" were made or to comply with a mandatory evaluation ordered by the courts.

These types of issues have been debated within the literature. Some theorists contend that couples therapy is not indicated when spouses refuse to give up an extramarital affair or are adamant about divorce alternatives (Schmaling, Fruzzetti, & Jacobson, 1989). This, of course, must be left to the discretion of the treating therapist. Sometimes situations that at first appear hopeless to either partner or to the treating therapist may indeed prove to be promising after all. It is recommended that all criteria be weighed carefully prior to making any decision to work with a particular case. (See Chapter 6 for further discussion.)

Often, couples will wait until the relationship is in extremely desperate straits before coming in for couples therapy. In fact, in some cases, it is too late to really make any effective change due to the amount and level of deterioration in the relationship. In these cases, a decision should be made as quickly as possible. In other cases, however, it may be overly pessimistic to simply not accept couples for treatment because of what may appear to be hopeless circumstances. Therapy often can provide some direction for the couple if several sessions are scheduled to decide on a course of action.

Booster sessions may also be used while adjunctive treatment is in process. For example, if one partner has a severe personality disorder, but nonetheless both partners want to do what they can to salvage the relationship, it may be plausible to see them for supportive couples therapy until some progress can be made in other therapies (e.g., individual).

ESTABLISHING A TREATMENT CONTRACT

Once both partners have been seen in individual sessions, they are seen again conjointly. It is important to note that if more than one individual visit is required to gather the information needed with one or both partners, that visit should be scheduled prior to the second conjoint visit. As an alternative to this, the therapist may want to schedule 90-minute sessions for the individual interviews in order to accelerate the intake process. Also, if insufficient information has been gathered in the first three sessions, then the assessment phase should be extended until the therapist has all the information needed.

The second conjoint visit should be a summary session in which the therapist ties all of the results of the previous evaluative sessions together and uses the information to develop a case conceptualization and a plan of action. This summary includes presenting the couple with a conceptualization of the case and a delineation of the problem areas. Some decision should be made by the therapist about the course of treatment at the culmination of the individual interviews. This is presented in the fourth meeting or what would be the second conjoint visit. Depending on how confident the therapist feels at this point, he or she may also want to share a professional opinion regarding an overall prognosis of the relationship and how amenable he or she feels the couple are to treatment.

This is also the session in which the therapist will begin to orient the couple to the cognitive model in an educational fashion (see Chapter 4, "Techniques and Procedures"). During this session the therapist should also emphasize the need for the treatment to involve a "collaborative set." This concept (Jacobson & Margolin, 1979), mentioned in Chapter 2, refers to the couple as a unit in which they view their relationship difficulties as a common problem that will only improve if they direct their efforts conjointly. Once the therapist ascertains the couple's willingness to collaborate, the therapist asks the couple if they wish to make a verbal commitment to treatment. (See Chapter 4 for approaches which are helpful with couples when a collaborative set is not readily achieved.)

IDENTIFYING PROBLEM AREAS

Usually, when a couple arrive for therapy, they are goal-directed - that is, they have at least some idea of what they want to see change in their relationship. This, however, varies from couple to couple with extremes ranging from partners who are keenly centered on problem areas to partners who are extremely vague and noncommunicative with respect to the types of problems that exist.

The use of the questionnaire *Problems in the Partnership* (Beck, 1988), or an alternative (those mentioned earlier in this chapter), may be useful at this stage, particularly when couples tend to be vague or nonspecific or even "clam up" when asked to define their problem areas. These questionnaires should be distributed at the end of the initial conjoint visit with instructions to complete them for the subsequently scheduled individual sessions. It is best that couples complete the forms separately and avoid discussing their answers.

As mentioned previously, the second and third sessions involve a solo interview with each member of the couple. During these interviews the therapist has the chance to probe specific areas of discontent and utilize the marital questionnaires and inventories to pinpoint and conceptualize problem areas. This is one of the first steps in actually conceptualizing the disturbance in the relationship. If the couple are clear about their areas of distress, then these will be supported by their answers on the questionnaires, allowing the therapist to firm up his or her conceptualization of their situation.

In determining which areas to focus on initially, the therapist should collaborate with the couple to choose which problems are most pressing. Often, if there has been a crisis (e.g., an extramarital affair exposed or violent acting-out behavior), this crisis may take precedence over other issues, such as communication. On the other hand, if no crisis is present, then the conceptualization (Persons, 1989) and issues raised in the individual sessions may serve as some indication of target areas to address (see Chapter 6 for more discussion on crises).

Once problem areas are identified, the therapist and couple should collaboratively rank order them in terms of their importance to the couple and debilitating effects on the relationship. Then the therapist and couple can begin addressing each problem area in turn.

IDENTIFYING COUPLES' AUTOMATIC THOUGHTS

One of the first steps in facilitating change with couples is to identify their automatic thoughts. As explained in Chapter 1, automatic thoughts are thoughts that occur to an individual spontaneously in situations as a result of an internal event. These thoughts may cause a person to feel and act in certain ways, including ways that can create conflict in relationships. Although this definition may portray automatic thoughts as easy to capture, they are not always so readily accessible and are sometimes difficult to identify.

The therapist must rely on certain techniques in the evaluative process to pinpoint these automatic thoughts and then should teach the clients to recognize them for themselves. The most direct way to identify automatic thoughts about the relationship is to define a specific situation and ask the client, "What is going through your mind right now?" Imagery can be used to help recapture the situation and possible thoughts as in the following example:

Miles: She just yells at me when I come home, tells me I'm inconsiderate. I hate that. So then I get mad.
Therapist: What goes through your mind when you get mad?
Miles: I don't know. It just makes me mad.
Therapist: What about it makes you mad?
Miles: Just her criticizing me.
Therapist: And what does that mean to you?
Miles: I'm not sure I know what you mean.
Therapist: Okay, let's see if we can figure out together what goes through your mind when you think Jackie is criticizing you. Can you imagine the scene when you get home?
Miles: Yeah.
Therapist: Do you imagine better with your eyes open or closed?
Miles: Closed, I guess.
Therapist: Okay, close your eyes and imagine the scene the last time you came home and Jackie yelled at you.

27

Miles:	I came in the kitchen and said, "Hi, babe? How's it going?" And then I picked up the paper to see who won the game and she started yelling at me.

(The therapist now asks Miles a number of questions about the sounds and sights to enhance his memory of the scene.)

Therapist:	So you are reading the paper and Jackie says you're inconsiderate and you look up and she has a hurt look on her face and she's saying, "You didn't even ask about our baby's checkup today!"
Miles:	Yeah.
Therapist:	How are you feeling right now?
Miles:	Like a jerk, but mad too.
Therapist:	What are you mad about?
Miles:	She's worried enough about the baby for both of us! It was just a 2-week checkup. I figured if the baby was sick she would have called me on the job. She has no right to call me inconsiderate for such a little slip up. She acts like I'm a complete failure as a husband!
Therapist:	And just before you got mad, when you felt like a jerk, what was going through your mind then?
Miles:	I thought, "Hey, here I was bragging to my buddies at work what a great dad I am and I completely forgot about the checkup."
Therapist:	Did that make you upset with yourself?
Miles:	Yeah, 'cuz I told myself I wasn't going to be like my dad.
Therapist:	And did this make you think you were like your dad?
Miles:	Yeah (clenching his fists).
Therapist:	What went through your mind just then?
Miles:	I saw my dad reading the racing form when I was trying to tell him about my baseball game.
Therapist:	How do you feel when you have that memory?
Miles:	Mad, I guess.
Therapist:	So you have lots of thoughts and feelings when we slow things down and look.
Miles:	Yeah, I guess so.
Therapist:	Let's look at some of those thoughts and feelings and see if they are connected somehow.

In this dialogue, the therapist asks Miles several times to re-call aspects of a specific situation and then to notice his thoughts and feelings. By asking "What was going through your mind right now" instead of "What were you thinking," the therapist leaves the door open for Miles to recall images and memories as well as word thoughts. It is important to capture any images or memories since these can be particularly potent sources of affect. Beck (personal communication, January, 1986) has called the question "What is going through your mind right now" the fundamental cognitive probe for identifying automatic thoughts.

USING AUTOMATIC THOUGHTS TO UNCOVER UNDERLYING BELIEFS (SCHEMAS)

During the excavation of a historical site, archaeologists uti-lize specific tools for unearthing artifacts. Because this process involves tedious maneuvers, the tools are usually specifically de-signed to remove soil in a delicate yet effective fashion in at-tempts to protect the artifact.

This example is analogous to the cognitive therapist's work in uncovering underlying beliefs or schemas. The tools used in this case are the basic elements of counseling and psychotherapy; namely, clarification, reflection, and establishing an effective rapport. Probably the tool of most precision, however, is ques-tioning. Questioning is the method used for uncovering automat-ic thoughts and underlying beliefs.

As defined previously, automatic thoughts are those thoughts that occur spontaneously in an individual's mind. They may be based on distorted information or erroneous logic. Questioning assists the therapist in uncovering automatic thoughts of which the individual may or may not be aware.

The process of identifying each individual's automatic thoughts is the therapist's avenue toward uncovering the underly-ing beliefs about the relationship and, most importantly, beliefs about change. To clarify the relationship between the two, automatic thoughts are applications of an idea or a product of an opinion. Underlying beliefs, on the other hand, are the ideas or opinions accepted as true which house the automatic thoughts. It is these underlying beliefs which govern how each partner thinks and subsequently interacts with his or her spouse. Therefore, a significant amount of time is dedicated to identifying these thoughts and beliefs, because these tell us the most about how individuals govern themselves.

29

Initially, automatic thoughts and underlying beliefs are identified during the individual interviews in order to avoid interference from the partner or reluctance to acknowledge deeply held beliefs. Later, it is recommended that the couple actually observe how they each think and identify their thoughts and beliefs by sharing automatic thoughts during conjoint sessions.

The following is a dialogue which was excerpted from an individual session. In this case, the therapist chose to focus on some of the items that the husband had marked on the *Beliefs About Change Questionnaire* (Beck, 1988). It differs from the previous scenario in that it aims to discover the underlying belief instead of simply identifying spontaneous automatic thoughts.

Therapist: John, I see that on the *Beliefs About Change Questionnaire* under "Defeatist Beliefs," you placed a check mark next to the statement, "My partner is incapable of change." What are your automatic thoughts about that statement?

John: Well, you see, it was a mutual decision for both of us to come here for counseling; however, I really do not believe that my spouse is capable of changing her ways, although she may act motivated to do so when in your presence.

Therapist: Then your thought is that although she appears motivated, there is little likelihood that she will change?

John: Yes, it's almost a waste of time.

Therapist: Any other thoughts about it?

John: Yes, I also think that I will be placed in a position of expending a lot of energy toward making the relationship work, and then the joke will be on me when we still end up getting separated.

Therapist: So your belief then is that going ahead in couples therapy will only result in making a fool of you?

John: Yes, I do and, therefore, I am reluctant to believe her when she says that she wants to try.

Therapist: What is your belief about change?

John: Well, basically, if you want to know the truth, I honestly feel that people basically remain the way they are, even though they might state that they wish to change. I believe in the old adage, "A leopard never changes its spots."

Therapist: I see. Then your underlying belief is that change is impossible; therefore, nothing can improve your relationship?

In this example, the therapist persists at questioning the automatic thoughts that are perceived to be indicative of how the husband views his relationship. The target of this, of course, is to tap into the underlying belief system. The core of John's belief in the preceding example is that "Change is impossible." While extremely important for the therapist to know, this belief may have not surfaced unless skillfully uncovered during the initial assessment. The therapist is now more aware of what he or she faces, which may help him or her steer clear of later difficulties in treatment. Moreover, it gives the therapist a window into how individuals view themselves and their relationship.

IDENTITY FROM FAMILY OF ORIGIN

The system theorists speak strongly about family of origin because they believe that it plays a major role in how individuals view their own relationships (Aylmer, 1986).

Issues from the families of origin of each spouse are important to cognitive therapists in the respect that they often shape central themes in the beliefs about the relationship. It is not uncommon when working with couples to frequently hear such statements as, "Well, this is what my mother always did" or "My parents rarely needed to discuss things."

It is strongly recommended that therapists spend time investigating some of the couple's recollections of their parents' relationships. This will help the couple better understand some of their own interactional patterns and begin to take steps toward modifications. Many individuals still firmly believe that because their parents did things a certain way, this is law and they must follow suit. It is no wonder then, that when their own relationships begin to fail or enter into conflict, they become easily frustrated and often puzzled as to why certain ways worked for their parents, but not for them. The difference, of course, may relate to an era or period in time or perhaps an unspoken agreement that existed between a certain couple. What's important, however, is that it must be made clear that partners may have to relinquish their beliefs about what worked or does work for other members of their family of origin and adopt new guidelines for themselves. This also will help reinforce the notion of getting in

31

touch with each other's needs and the importance of gaining a better understanding of their partner. This can be achieved through the cognitive restructuring process explained in detail in Chapter 4.

Therapists should use the information they obtain during sessions and actively point out to partners when they are drawing on beliefs derived from a family of origin. These beliefs should then be evaluated as to how functional they are in the current situation and whether they should be maintained or abandoned for new ones. If beliefs are determined to be obsolete, then the emphasis can be placed on adopting new belief systems that work for this couple.

When the initial assessment phase has been completed, a conceptualization of the case is formed, along with a plan of treatment. This should be abridged and shared with the couple in nonclinical terms which they can clearly comprehend. Following this, the couple should be oriented to the Cognitive Therapy model.

Evaluator:_____   Date:_____

CLINICIAN'S INTAKE EVALUATION FOR COUPLES*

I. **Identifying Data**

Patient Name_____

Sex_____   Age_____   Race_____

Occupational Status_____   Religion_____

Patient Name_____

Sex_____   Age_____   Race_____

Occupational Status_____   Religion_____

Relationship Status (circle):

    Engaged   Married   Separated   Remarried

    Divorced   Cohabiting   Commuter Relationship

Length of time married (length of relationship if not married):

_____

Children:

Name	Age	Sex	Living at Home

*This instrument was developed by, and reproduced with permission of, the Center for Cognitive Therapy, Room 602, 133 South 36th Street, Philadelphia, PA 19104. Reprinted by permission.

II. **Presenting Problems** (get both partners' reports):

Partner 1	Partner 2
Name_____	Name_____
1. What is the major problem?	1. What is the major problem?
2. Symptoms?	2. Symptoms?
a: Affective:	a: Affective:
b: Physiological:	b: Physiological:
c: Cognitive:	c: Cognitive:
d: Behavioral:	d: Behavioral:
3. How long have you had this problem?	3. How long have you had this problem?
4. Similar problems in the past?	4. Similar problems in the past?

5. a: Occur most?

    b: Most severe?

6. What thoughts?

7. Images?

8. Any situation when it
    does not occur?

9. Do you know why?

10. What have you done to
    help?

5. a: Occur most?

    b: Most severe?

6. What thoughts?

7. Images?

8. Any situation when it
    does not occur?

9. Do you know why?

10. What have you done to
    help?

11. Any ideas of harming self? (Suicidal Ideation)
11. Any ideas of harming self? (Suicidal Ideation)

12. Any ideas of harming others?
12. Any ideas of harming others?

Note: When couples break into <u>individual</u> assessment, therapist asks:

13. Is there any answer that you would change now that your spouse is out of the room?
13. Is there any answer that you would change now that your spouse is out of the room?

III. **Joint Problems:**

1. Areas of conflict:

2. Communication problems:

3. Problem with others (children, parents):

4. Sexual problems:

5. Other areas of concern (individual problems which cause conflict, etc.):

6. Any history of physical violence:

IV. **Individual Diagnoses:**

<u>Partner 1</u>   Name_____

Axis I (Diagnosis)

_____

Axis II (Personality Characteristics)

_____

Axis III (Medical Problems)

_____

Axis IV (Psychosocial Stressors)

_____

Axis V (Highest Adaptive Functioning)

_____

Partner 2   Name_____

Axis I (Diagnosis)

_____

Axis II (Personality Characteristics)

_____

Axis III (Medical Problems)

_____

Axis IV (Psychosocial Stressors)

_____

Axis V (Highest Adaptive Functioning)

_____

V. **Treatment Recommendations:**

_____   _____
Signature of Inverviewer   Consultant Signature

4.
TECHNIQUES AND PROCEDURES

EDUCATING COUPLES
TO THE COGNITIVE MODEL

Educating the couple to the model of treatment is important, particularly for cognitive therapists. With a mode of treatment that involves such a structured and collaborative approach, it is essential that the couple understand clearly the principles and methods involved. This is particularly important because the therapist will constantly be referring back to the model and making references to specific concepts. Knowing and reviewing the model also keeps both spouses more attuned to what is going on with them during the process of treatment and reinforces the notion of taking responsibility for their own thoughts and actions.

The educational process usually occurs initially during the second conjoint session; however, it can be addressed again at any point in the therapy. It is advised that this be done during a conjoint session so both members of the couple receive the same information. The model is usually explained in terms similar to the statement below:

Cognitive Therapy is based on a model that our biology, mood, behavior, thinking, and environment all interact. For example, if our mood is depressed, our behavior decreases, our thinking is negative, and our biology changes. With couples, your environment (history, family structure, pressures, etc.), health, moods, behavior, and

39

thinking all interact. To improve your relationship, therefore, we have to see what we can do in each of those five areas to help you feel better and get along better.

One important area of Cognitive Therapy with Couples involves helping couples become aware of the dysfunctional thoughts that they have in their relationship, and which lead to conflict. The expectations you bring to the relationship will be a primary focus of therapy. Dysfunctional relationships often result when one or both partners hold distorted beliefs or unrealistic expectations about themselves and the relationship. Over time, couples often come to negative conclusions about each other's behaviors which can lead to seeing each other in an exclusively negative light. You can then tend to focus more on each other's negative behaviors, failing to notice the positives. This may hurl you into a continuous spiral of conflicting interaction until you are constantly arguing or ignoring each other completely.

Cognitive Therapy with couples uses a set of principles and techniques that are designed to shift and expand your perspectives in interpreting the meanings and causes of your behaviors. In addition, I will teach you ways to communicate and solve problems that can work better than your current pattern. It is through these techniques that you can learn to correct your faulty interactions and improve your relationship.

The therapist may choose, at his or her discretion, to add to or subtract from the detail of this summary or to spread it out over the course of several sessions. This information should be delivered in language matching the vocabulary level of the couple. The couple may also be requested to supplement their understanding of the model by reading books such as *Love Is Never Enough* (Beck, 1988), or, for a more general understanding of Cognitive Therapy, the *Feeling Good Handbook* by David Burns (1989). Bibliotherapy works best if the therapist selects a few pages or a chapter that summarizes information already discussed in therapy. In general, clients should not be handed a book to read and be expected to understand its relevance to therapy unless the therapist discusses it with them before and after. It is also important to explain to the couple that homework assignments will be an important part of treatment.

In addition to this, there are a number of points which should be highlighted after explaining the model. The need for the therapist to structure the sessions is crucial and, therefore, should be explained in detail. Very often couples who are in distress tend to resist structure by the therapist, particularly when they are in the middle of a crisis. It is therefore important that the therapist stress that he or she will always move toward structuring the sessions in an attempt to remain on target with the treatment process. Part of the structuring process involves setting agendas. The agenda is usually set by both the therapist and the couple at the beginning of each session in order to map out the course of the sessions. This also helps to guard against straying away from the pertinent issues in treatment (see Chapter 5).

This is also the best time to establish ground rules in treatment (e.g., phone calls will be kept to a minimum except for crises). It is not uncommon for a couples' therapist to struggle with such issues as partner domination, whereby one of the couple attempts to repeatedly contact the therapist by phone outside of the sessions to control the therapy process. Another common dilemma is where one partner accuses the therapist of siding with the spouse and not treating their case objectively. This is where ground rules in treatment may serve to protect all parties during the treatment process.

Once the therapist believes that the couple have gained a fairly good working knowledge of the model, and have accepted the ground rules, it is then time to begin to actively familiarize them with the notion of cognitive distortions and how to identify them.

Although cognitive distortions do exist in many different facets of an individual's functioning, the specific distortions that are the focus in couples' treatment are on the relationship itself. Very often distortions that pertain to issues outside of the relationship may emerge. These may have to be handled more on an individual basis, particularly if they are not germane to the relationship. This is a judgment call on the part of the therapist because such thoughts may or may not arbitrarily contribute to relationship dysfunction.

As described earlier, there are a number of cognitive distortions in which couples frequently engage. Identifying these distortions and labeling them are an important part of the restructuring aspect of treatment. The next section will introduce the concept of cognitive distortions and how to teach partners to identify them.

IDENTIFYING COGNITIVE
DISTORTIONS AND LABELING THEM

Because cognitive distortions are an integral part of the therapy process, it is essential that the couple learn not only to recognize them, but also to identify them readily. An essential part of treatment then is for the therapist to make sure the couple understand this clearly. One exercise is to have each partner keep a log of negative thoughts during the week and label any distortions in those thoughts. This log should be reviewed by the individual and the therapist until the individual can do this exercise successfully. This will be important later when it will be necessary for the therapist to rely on the couple's ability to recognize and identify distortions. When the couple come in for their sessions, the log of negative thoughts should be reviewed with both partners identifying the distortions described on the following pages.

The time spent on this topic is important because otherwise many distortions will be considered true by individuals. For example: A man whose spouse spends more than the amount of money he feels is necessary for household items may honestly believe his spouse is acting out against him. He may view her actions as direct retaliation against his demands when, in fact, it may not be related at all.

Identifying cognitive distortions involves a type of self-monitoring that is imperative in Cognitive Therapy for restructuring thought processes. The same cognitive distortions that were introduced in early writings on Cognitive Therapy (Beck, Rush, et al., 1979) are applied in treating couples. Below is a list of 10 of the most common cognitive distortions made by couples:

1. *Arbitrary Inference.* Conclusions are made in the absence of supporting substantiating evidence. For example, a man whose wife arrives home a half-hour late from work concludes, "She must be having an affair."

2. *Selective Abstraction.* Information is taken out of context; certain details are highlighted while other important information is ignored. For example, a woman whose husband fails to answer her greeting the first thing in the morning concludes, "He must be angry at me again."

3. *Overgeneralization.* An isolated incident or two is allowed to serve as a representation of similar situations every-

where, related or unrelated. For example, after being turned down for an initial date, a young man concludes, "All women are alike: I'll always be rejected."

4. *Magnification and Minimization.* A case or circumstance is perceived in greater or lesser light than is appropriate. For example, an angry husband "blows his top" upon discovering that the checkbook is unreconciled and states to his wife, "We're financially doomed."

5. *Personalization.* External events are attributed to oneself when insufficient evidence exists to render a conclusion. For example, a woman finds her husband re-ironing an already pressed shirt and assumes, "He is dissatisfied with me."

6. *Dichotomous Thinking.* Experiences are codified as either all or nothing, a complete success or a total failure. This is otherwise known as "polarized thinking." For example, a wife's opinion on a paperhanging job underway in the recreation room is solicited, and, after she questions the seams, the husband thinks to himself, "I can't do anything right."

7. *Labeling and Mislabeling.* Imperfections and mistakes made in the past are allowed to define one's self. For example, subsequent to continual mistakes in meal preparation, a partner states, "I am worthless," as opposed to recognizing the errors as being human.

8. *Tunnel Vision.* Sometimes partners see only what they want to see or what fits their current state of mind. A man who believes that his lover "does whatever he wants anyway" may accuse him of making a choice based on purely selfish reasons.

9. *Biased Explanations.* This is an almost suspicious type of thinking that partners develop during times of distress, during which there is an automatic assumption that their mate holds a negative ulterior motive for actions. For example: A woman states to herself, "He's acting real 'lovey-dovey' because he'll later probably want me to do something that he knows I hate to do."

10. *Mind Reading.* This is the magical gift of being able to know what the other is thinking without the aid of verbal communication. Couples end up ascribing negative intentions to their partners. For example: A man thinks to himself, "I know what is going through her mind, she thinks that I am naïve to her 'shenanigans.'"

These distortions have been found to occur frequently among couples in distress and, in fact, may occur for the most part with every relationship at one time or another.

Couples are made aware of these common distortions and then instructed to identify where their own thinking may fit with these distortions. Each time a person experiences an automatic thought about his or her partner and identifies it as a negative or dysfunctional thought, he or she then attempts to label it as one of the previous distortions. When couples learn to assign a label to their cognitive distortions, they are then able to set the stage for re-evaluating the structure of their thinking.

It should be made clear at this point that the expertise of the clinician is important in determining whether or not additional psychopathology is evident in an individual's thought process (see Chapter 3). If not detected during the assessment phase, any disorder in thinking, behavior, or affect may clearly manifest itself here. Should this be the case, alternative types of treatment may need to be considered. Depending on whether or not the problem is severe, couples therapy may or may not be discontinued.

For example: A couple married almost 35 years initiated Cognitive Therapy after reading an article in a popular health magazine. During the course of treatment, while learning to identify distorted thoughts, it became clear to the therapist that there was an overly suspicious tenor in the wife's concerns for her husband. When probed further, her suspicions took on a paranoid flavor accompanied by a gradual decompensation in functioning as she was questioned in depth. As a result, the woman was referred to a psychiatrist for an evaluation, and the couple were advised to temporarily discontinue marital counseling until stabilization could be maintained with the wife.

When there are no severe interfering problems, the partners are instructed to keep track of their automatic thoughts and begin to identify the distortions by labeling them. The following is an example:

Automatic Thoughts and Cognitive Distortions

Automatic Thought	Label
"My husband should know by now that I hate chick-peas in my salad."	Mind Reading

Automatic Thought	Label
"It's too late to do any- thing about this marriage." "It's dead on arrival."	Magnification

The purpose of these exercises is for the couple to recognize that their thinking may be distorted due to insufficient information and to help them monitor the kind and frequency of distortions they use. This conscious monitoring of their thoughts and distortions enables them to become more aware of how their thinking affects their partner and themselves.

FAULTY INFORMATION PROCESSING

Cognitive theorists believe dysfunctional thinking and distortions develop from faulty information processing. It is believed that individuals learn maladaptive ways of processing information as a result of exposure to their environment and also due to a biological tendency to categorize and group observations. These processes involve perceptions of, and inferences made from, certain stimuli. The stereotypic scenario of a woman who is afraid of a mouse illustrates this process. Every time she comes in contact with a mouse, regardless of its size, the cartoon woman begins to scream irrationally and climbs for the highest ground. Her underlying belief or schema is that mice are something to be fearful of. If questioned, she might say she is uncertain as to exactly why, but it is something that she has been raised to believe; she almost instinctually fears mice. If pressed, she may disclose to you that she learned through a parent that mice are dirty or contaminated with germs. Yet, this still leaves insufficient information to support such an exaggerated fear reaction. This is an example of a belief that is supported by insufficient or faulty information - or a distorted belief. It is devoid of substantiating information.

NEGATIVE FRAMING

It is interesting to note that the complaints of couples during the intake phase often include particular characteristics of their partners that are the inverse, negative side of those characteristics that once attracted them to their partner (Abrahms & Spring, 1989). For example, in the case of Barbara and Steve, Barbara stated that the characteristics of Steve she finds to be most intolerable are that he is lazy, demanding, picky, and absent-minded. Ironically, when asked later for some of the characteristics that attracted Barbara to Steve, she listed the following adjectives: laid back, knows his expectations of others, precise, and carefree.

When these characteristics were listed juxtaposed on paper, Barbara could clearly see that her negative impressions of Steve were merely the negative side of what she at one time viewed as being positive characteristics. Following is an example outlined:

Initial Redeeming Qualities of Steve		Current Irritating Qualities of Steve
Laid-back	----------------	Lazy
Knows his expectations of others	----------------	Demanding
Precise	----------------	Picky
Carefree	----------------	Absent-minded
Amorous	----------------	Always wants sex

Outlining this concept serves as a powerful tool for couples to begin to accept the notion of negative framing and how the negative frame itself is often merely a distortion of what were once considered attractive qualities. This perspective often gives individuals some hope, and it also encourages them to investigate their distortions. More importantly, they can begin to change their perceptions by questioning the evidence for their thinking.

Once couples accept the concept of negative framing, it can reinforce the cognitive model. This technique is used with both partners, preferably during a conjoint session. Alternatively, it might be constructed during an individual session, and then reviewed during a conjoint session with an emphasis on demonstrating for the spouse the process of restructuring the negative frame to a more positive frame.

TEACHING COUPLES TO IDENTIFY AUTOMATIC THOUGHTS

The crux of the cognitive model of relationship therapy is the identification of partners' automatic thoughts about themselves and, most importantly, about the relationship. Once again, automatic thoughts are defined as thoughts which occur spontaneously in the individual's mind about certain life circumstances or individuals in the environment. These automatic thoughts may be either negative or positive; however, in most conflictual situations, they are negative. Some of the most common negative automatic thoughts include:

- "If he loved me, then he would spend more time with me."
- "She only cares about herself."
- "The relationship is hopeless."
- "Nothing I do pleases him."
- "I can't do anything right."

By teaching couples to observe their thinking and their patterns of thought, they develop the skill of identifying automatic thoughts that spontaneously flash through their minds. These are the cognitions that can trigger emotional responses and behavioral actions which often cause conflict.

Since many of these automatic thoughts arise from underlying beliefs that have developed slowly over time, they are corrected and restructured over time through the use of identification and practice. In lay terms, such identification allows individuals to "think about what they are telling themselves" about the situation or circumstance.

In order to improve the skill of identifying automatic thoughts, clients are typically instructed to keep a pad or notebook handy and to jot down a brief description of the circumstances surrounding a conflict period. Included in this notation should be a description of the situation, the automatic thought that came to mind, and the resulting emotional response. A modified version of the "Daily Dysfunctional Thought Record" (Center for Cognitive Therapy, Philadelphia) may be used for this purpose. Below is an example of excerpts extrapolated from clients' notebooks:

Relevant Situation/Event	Automatic Thought	Emotional Response
"Karen overdrew our checking account by several hundred dollars."	"She has no concept of budgeting whatsoever."	Frustration

Relevant Situation/Event	Automatic Thought	Emotional Response
	"This is her subtle little way of forcing me to bring home more money."	Anger and Resentment
"Todd failed to take out the trash again last night."	"He really expects me to do this job."	Resentful
	"He thinks he's too good to stoop to such a menial task."	Anger/ Belittled

Through this type of record keeping, the therapist is able to demonstrate to the couple how their automatic thoughts are linked to emotional responses and how this contributes to their negative frame of their mate.

LINKING EMOTIONS WITH AUTOMATIC THOUGHTS

Once spouses have learned to accurately identify automatic thoughts, more emphasis is placed on linking thoughts to emotional responses. This is important because it has been found that, very often, impulsive behaviors that create damage in relationships occur as a result of charged emotions. In addition, spouses will often chalk up certain experiences or situations as a result of "just how they feel," disowning any responsibility for being able to influence how they feel. For example, one husband stated that he failed to see the use in trying to work out his marital problems because he simply did not feel emotion for his wife anymore. This emotion can be linked to certain automatic thoughts which may explain more clearly why his feeling is blunted.

An exercise that often proves quite useful for couples is to have them review their log books and indicate the links between thought and emotion. Then they use a method of alternative responding or thought correction to effect emotional change.

THE USE OF IMAGERY
AND ROLE PLAY TECHNIQUES

When identifying their automatic thoughts and underlying beliefs, couples may sometimes have difficulty recalling pertinent information regarding conflict areas, particularly during emotionally charged situations. Imagery and/or role play techniques may be extremely helpful in jogging memories regarding such situations. In addition, these techniques may also be useful in helping partners revive their feelings about one another (see scenario in Chapter 3, pp. 27-28). The use of fantasy recollection to revive old emotion toward one another during dating periods may help couples see that those feelings were there at one time and may be regenerated depending on their efforts in working on the relationship.

Therapists can utilize these techniques throughout therapy. They may be useful in the early stages of therapy, when one or both partners are claiming they cannot recall happier times. The therapist may suggest to one or both (in a conjoint visit or individually) to focus on past scenes or images, such as early anniversaries, birthdays, their wedding day, dating periods, and so forth. This imagery session may be more successful if the therapist has the individuals focus specifically on what they or their partner were wearing at the time, what the room was like that they were in, specific recollection of other people who were present, and so on. Details such as these may serve to jog memories of old feelings. These exercises are meant to serve as primers of motivation to rekindle positive feelings, or feelings believed to be lost. Once the therapist is able to facilitate a positive image with the individuals, then they can begin to link emotions and positive automatic thoughts to those images.

Imagery techniques are certainly not for everyone and may even backfire at times, depending on the individual. Therefore, they should be used with caution. Role play techniques are also used to flush out feelings or thoughts, particularly in those couples who are noncommunicative in therapy or treatment sessions. The therapist should use discretion in determining when these techniques are appropriate.

DISPELLING AUTOMATIC THOUGHTS
AND REFRAMING/TESTING
AUTOMATIC THOUGHTS

The process of restructuring automatic thoughts involves considering alternative explanations and adopting them as part of the individual's cognitive repertoire. In order to accomplish this, the dysfunctional automatic thought has to be tested by the client. Once this is accomplished, a reframing of perception occurs which may allow the client to view his or her partner or situation in a different light.

An example of this is a woman who developed the belief that her husband was no longer in love with her as a result of his withdrawal. Her thoughts occurred in the following sequence:

Automatic Thought	Emotion	Cognitive Distortion
1. "Bob has been increasingly withdrawn from me over the past week and a half. This has to mean something about our relationship."	Worried	Personalization
2. "I don't think he loves me anymore."	Sad/ Depressed	Mind Reading Arbitrary Inference

In the example above, Automatic Thought #1 is accompanied by an emotion of worry and is an example of personalization because she interprets Bob's behavior as relating only to herself. In fact, it is possible he may be withdrawing from everyone. She then draws an arbitrary inference from what she observes and makes a global negative statement, "He doesn't love me anymore."

The next step is to ask her to test her thoughts by weighing the existing evidence and considering alternative explanations. For example:

What evidence exists to substantiate this thought?	Might there be an alternative explanation for this behavior?
1. "He doesn't appear to be excited to see me when I come home."	1. "Perhaps something else is bothering him. Work or finances maybe."
2. "He is less amorous than he used to be with me."	2. "He might just need some space from me right now - time to breathe."

By weighing the evidence that exists and seeing that it actually is insufficient to draw any strong conclusion, the individual is able to consider an alternative explanation. This will very likely reduce her negative frame until she has the opportunity to gather additional data. She can collect additional data by observing for a longer period of time or inquiring, in a nonthreatening manner, what may be causing him to withdraw. The latter, of course, may also require communication training for both spouses. This exercise will at least help set the tone for her approach, making her inquiry to him much less accusatory.

RATING THE ALTERNATIVE EXPLANATION OR ALTERNATIVE RESPONSE

Individuals should subsequently rate their belief in the alternative explanation. This is important because it may not become assimilated as a new part of their thinking unless they place some degree of belief in it. For example, with the woman in the previous scenario, on a scale of 0%-100%, she rated her alternative beliefs 50%.

Rating of This Belief

I believe that this may be 50% true.

As time progresses, the therapist should look for an increase in the percentage of the belief rate if new evidence supports it.

THE USE OF DOWNWARD ARROW

Downward arrow (Beck, Rush, et al., 1979) is a technique used to track the anticipated outcome of automatic thoughts so couples can evaluate whether the expected catastrophe is likely

51

to happen. It is also used to identify the underlying assumptions beneath one's automatic thoughts and to uncover the "hidden fears." This is done by identifying the initial thought: "I really screwed up," and asking the individual, "If so, then what?"

As in the example of the woman who was concerned with her husband's low opinion of her, the following depiction of the use of downward arrow describes the sequence of her thoughts, and her core or hidden belief.

"I screwed up the checkbook balance
for the third time in 2 months."

"Only an idiot would make such a
blunder like this."

"This will really certify me as an
idiot in John's (husband) eyes."

"What in God's name does he want
with someone like me anyway?"

"Once he realizes this, he'll
probably dump me."

It is clear how making errors in the checkbook register was such a crucial event for this woman. The use of downward arrow technique demonstrates how her thinking leads to a questioning of her husband's true need for her. This technique allows both the therapist and the individual to see the chaining of thoughts and how they lead to erroneous conclusions and reinforce distorted beliefs. Moreover, it aids in identifying that the underlying issue is her low self-esteem and sense of inadequacy.

The therapist can use downward arrow in as many steps as desired and have the individual discontinue at the point when the therapist and client feel the core belief has been reached. Ideally, both partners will adopt and use this technique on their own.

THE USE OF EVIDENCE IN
CORRECTING DISTORTED THINKING

As mentioned earlier, when restructuring thought processes and underlying beliefs, it is essential to help the individual learn to rely on evidence to support the correction of distorted thoughts. It is the collection of evidence that allows an individual to weigh contrasting information against that which is being used in formulating the individual's current thoughts and beliefs. Since most distorted thoughts come from faulty or erroneous information, then it stands that new competing evidence is required to test and change existing thoughts. Gathering and weighing the evidence for one's thoughts is an integral part of Cognitive Therapy.

WEIGHING THE EVIDENCE
AND TESTING PREDICTIONS

Weighing the evidence is actually a skill which needs to be developed over time. Just as a prosecuting attorney or a forensic pathologist needs to carefully weigh each piece of evidence prior to rendering a decision or gathering more data, each partner must act in a similar manner. In spending time to review each piece of information, the individual has time to carefully consider its validity. Writing this down is especially helpful for the individual to see what actually is known.

The other side of restructuring is testing predictions. When the evidence appears insufficient, it is often a good idea to formulate a hypothesis, think about what might occur in any given situation, and test the prediction. This is another form of gathering data. For example, suppose the woman in the scenario earlier who feared rejection from her husband because she overdrew the checking account tested her prediction to see if her husband would actually reject her. She could intentionally question him about her fear and gather hard-core evidence in order to evaluate her thoughts and decide whether or not they are viable. Testing predictions is another means of dispelling dysfunctional thoughts.

PRACTICING ALTERNATIVE EXPLANATIONS

Just as couples have learned to govern themselves by distorted thinking through daily practice, they must relearn alternative modes of thinking based on the information gathered and practice these new thoughts daily. One step toward this end is to develop alternative explanations for actions and practice applying them. With repeated practice, couples can learn to restructure their thinking and balance out the distortions derived from faulty information. As a continual homework assignment, the therapist can have couples practice these alternative responses and explanations until they become adopted as a regular part of their thought processes. A schematic example of how this can occur (taken from a man's logbook) is found on page 55.

REFRAMING - CONSIDERING THE NEGATIVES IN A POSITIVE LIGHT

Reframing involves taking all of the data gathered, weighing the evidence, and developing alternative explanations and a new view of the partner. This then replaces the negative frame once held by the client. Another way to accomplish this is to view the negative attributes in a positive light. This should not be confused with "the power of positive thinking." By weighing actual evidence, it is instead a more systematic and confirmative way of viewing people or situations in a different and more realistic light. It is also something that does not happen overnight; couples should be cautioned to expect gradual change.

The therapist teaches couples to integrate all of the newly gathered data and practice viewing it cohesively. This process is clearly demonstrated in the case example in Chapter 7.

INCREASING POSITIVES IN THE RELATIONSHIP

In addition to cognitive interventions, Cognitive Therapy emphasizes behavioral change. Behavioral homework assignments may be given to couples at any point in treatment to improve the quality of the relationship, strengthen new skills, or test the validity of beliefs as described previously.

At the beginning of therapy, cognitive therapists often assign homework to couples to increase the positive interactions in their relationship. This type of behavioral assignment was first described in detail by Stuart (1980) as "Caring Days."

In the Caring Days intervention, the couple act toward each other "as if" they still loved each other as much as during the best times of their relationship. Each member of the couple writes out a list of positive, specific, small behaviors that they would like

Situation	Automatic Thought	Emotional Response	Weigh and Question Evidence	Hypothesis/ Prediction
"Karen overdrew our checkbook by several hundred dollars."	"She has no concept of budgeting whatsoever." "This is her subtle way of forcing me to bring home more money."	Frustration Anger and Resentment	"She overdrew the checkbook, but there is no other indication that she's bad at budgeting or wants more money from me."	"There is a good chance that she may have just made a mistake."

Gather More Evidence (Reframe)	Alternative Response	Emotional Response
Asks wife if she knew that the checkbook was overdrawn - She says no and seems surprised.	This is likely the case - It's not aimed at me - She made a mistake.	Less frustrated and angry - She made a mistake.

their partner to do for them. These small behaviors should be ones that have not been the center of conflict.

After review with the therapist, the couple exchange lists and agree to each do at least five things on the list for their partner daily. The rationale for this assignment can be given as follows:

> Early on in our relationships we have problems, but we also are receiving so many positive things from our partner that the rewards outweigh the difficulties. Over time, it is normal for couples to begin doing fewer and fewer little positives for each other. Therefore, in time, the problems begin to outweigh the positives, and we can begin to question the worth of our relationships.

> In this Caring Days exercise, you are going to do an experiment to find out what happens if you increase the positives in your relationship again. It is important you do these positives even if you don't feel like it or if you are angry. The commitment is for at least five positives per day. There is no requirement for how you feel toward your partner. Instead, we are going to see if the positive behaviors alone will begin to restore a positive foundation to your relationship so it seems more 'worthwhile' to you to solve your problems together.

This seemingly small exchange of positive behaviors can have a profound effect on a couple's relationship. Most couples find after 1 or 2 weeks of Caring Days that they feel more positive toward each other. There is often a spontaneous recall of other good times in the relationship. This behavioral experiment frequently helps set up a positive expectation for change. It also introduces collaboration into the couple's at-home interactions. Many couples choose to continue Caring Days even after it is no longer a therapy assignment.

COMMUNICATION TRAINING
AND PROBLEM SOLVING

Teaching more effective communication and methods for solving problems are basic components of most therapies for couples. As stated in Chapter 2, Cognitive Therapy draws on the methods developed by other, mostly behavioral, couples' therapists (Jacobson & Margolin, 1979; Stuart, 1980) to accomplish these goals. For a more detailed approach to couples communication see Gottman et al. (1976).

Since Cognitive Therapy is an educational approach, it is easy to incorporate communication training into the flow of therapy. By remaining alert to the beliefs that can interfere with good communication and problem solving, the cognitive therapist can combine traditional communication teaching methods with Cognitive Therapy approaches for identifying and testing important beliefs.

The following sections outline methods for teaching couples improved communication and problem-solving skills. Common beliefs are identified that can block couples from learning and practicing these skills. Methods for therapeutically responding to these beliefs are also described.

TEACHING COMMUNICATION SKILLS

Researchers have discovered that both therapists and couples cite communication difficulties as the most frequent and damaging problem in distressed relationships (Geiss & O'Leary, 1981). Many couples come to therapy saying: "We need to communicate better." Requests for help "communicating" often translate as: "I want my partner to understand me and agree with me, and I want things to go more smoothly." Often, therefore, the first task of the therapist is to help the couple understand that good communication does not necessarily imply agreement. Instead, good communication involves learning to speak and listen in ways that are conducive to mutual understanding and, ideally, mutual problem solving when there is disagreement. The first therapeutic goal, then, is to help the couple view communication as a mutual benefit process rather than a power struggle or debate. One of the best ways to accomplish this is to establish a standard communication exercise in which the couple take turns as speaker and listener. Each are coached in the qualities that constitute a good speaker and a good listener (Beck, 1988).

During the exercise, the therapist can intervene and actively guide the couple in areas where improvement is needed most. After this very structured communication exercise, the therapist can solicit feedback from the couple regarding how the experience was similar to or different from their usual discussions. It is important also for the couple to identify what they each liked about the exercise and the areas of difficulty.

The therapist can help the couple learn from this exercise the advantages of working as a team (each with different tasks depending on their respective roles). In the same manner, the therapist can help the couple discover that, although it is difficult to listen in this structured way, the payoff is that each partner can gain a better understanding of the other's concerns, and both can learn more about each other. This can help mutual problem solving and anger diffusion.

The dialogue below illustrates this process:

Therapist: Today, Pat and Chris, we planned to practice a different way of talking with each other. Is that still OK with you as our goal for the day?

Pat/Chris: Sure.

Therapist: We need to pick a topic to discuss. Is there anything relevant from this week or do you want to talk about one of the conflicts on our list from the past few sessions?

Chris: We've been arguing this week about what to do Saturday night - it might help to get that settled.

Therapist: Would that topic be OK for you Pat?

Pat: (Nods)

Therapist: OK. This may seem a bit artificial at first, but we're going to practice "talking and listening with rules" - much like in a sports match, where each player has to follow certain guidelines so the game goes fairly. First, let me lay out the rules: You are going to take turns being the Speaker and the Listener. The Speaker has a few rules and the Listener role is a little more complicated so I'll help coach the Listener. Who wants to be the Speaker first?

Pat: I will.

Therapist: Alright. Pat, as the Speaker you will try to explain to Chris what you think and feel about the Saturday night plans. Try to be brief - you know how it feels if someone goes on and on. Also, try to stay on target by talking about yourself and what you feel and want rather than talking about Chris. For example, instead of saying, "YOU never take my feelings into account," which would indicate blame, try saying, "I'D like you to hear my feelings. I feel . . . when you . . . ." Understand?

Pat: Yes.

Therapist: Now, Chris, you have the more difficult role first. As listener, you have two aims: First, you want to find out as much as possible about what Pat thinks and feels about the Saturday night plans. As a good listener, you will want to learn as much as you can. This can be difficult because Pat might say things you think are wrong or that make you mad. But, when in the listening role, you can't disagree or talk back with your ideas. Instead, you are going to listen and ask questions only - no comments. Do you understand?

Chris: Yes.

Therapist: Now, in addition, when we've done this for 5 minutes, I'm going to ask you, Chris, to summarize what Pat said to make sure you understand Pat's position completely. Pat will let you know if you left anything out. When we're finished, we'll switch roles and then you will have a chance to be the Speaker and Pat will be the Listener for your viewpoint. Are you both ready? (Nods). Pat, let's begin by you telling Chris what you think and feel about Saturday night.

Pat: Well, I . . . . (Pat outlines for 2 minutes her reasons for wanting to go out to dinner and a movie.)

Chris: But don't you think it would be just as much fun to stay home and watch a video? - We could order out for dinner.

Therapist: Wait! That first part was a question, Chris. But it wasn't a question aimed at learning more about Pat's views. It was similar to an attorney cross-examining a witness (both laugh). That's good - we've learned something. Not all questions help us listen. Some questions turn listening into a debate, which often sparks resentment. Try to ask something that truly shows interest in Pat's ideas, Chris.

Chris: I'm not sure what.

Therapist: Well, do you know how Pat feels when going out as compared to staying home?

Chris: How do you feel when we go out?

Pat: When we go out I feel special. Like it's a date and you want to be with me.

Chris: Don't you feel the same when we stay home?

Therapist: Good question, Chris. Now you're asking about Pat's experience. Pat?

59

Pat: Well, it's not the same. I work at home and so it's hard for me to get into a romantic mind-set if I'm there all day.

(Pat and Chris go back and forth for a few more minutes.)

Therapist: That's good. Chris, could you summarize to Pat what are the main ideas and feelings that you've heard?

Chris: Pat likes to go out because after working at home all week it's hard to feel romantic at home. Also, Pat feels closer to me when we're out because it seems I pay more attention then. Pat feels kind of lonely when I work late and then do chores on the weekend.

Therapist: Did Chris leave out anything important, Pat?

Pat: No. That's pretty much it.

Therapist: Was this the same or different from your dialogue this week?

Pat/Chris: Very different!

Therapist: How so?

Pat: We fought and became real angry with one another. I didn't feel Chris heard me before.

Therapist: Tell Chris what this felt like to you just now.

Pat: It felt good because you seemed to really listen to me. I feel less angry because for once I think you heard me.

Therapist: What was this like for you Chris?

Chris: It's hard to think of questions. And it's hard to not get mad or make a point when I disagree.

Therapist: Good. This is an important point - it is very hard to listen when we are not in agreement. Were there any advantages to listening anyway? Did you learn anything new?

Chris: I guess I never realized how hard it must be to be home all the time. I'm gone so much it feels good to stay put when I get there.

Pat: I've told you a million times that I go buggy at home!

Therapist: Right. But today Chris finally heard you. Chris, why do you think you heard Pat today better than the other times?

Chris: Usually when we talk about this I'm feeling criticized and I'm thinking more about my defense than what Pat's saying.

Therapist: Oh - that's important. Did Pat talk differently today?
Chris: Yes. More calmly and quietly.
Therapist: Pat, were you calmer and quieter because I am present or was it due to something else?
Pat: I didn't think I had to yell because I knew Chris was going to listen.
Therapist: So we've discovered a number of advantages of this type of "talking and listening by the rules." Would the two of you summarize for me what you have learned as the advantages of this over your typical style of communication.

(Pat and Chris summarize.)

Therapist: Good. Now let's switch roles and we're going to hear what Chris thinks and feels about Saturday night and I'm going to coach you Pat in how to listen and ask questions. When we're done, Pat can summarize Chris' view. Ready?

(The exercise is repeated with the therapist periodically pointing out good questions, helping Pat think of appropriate questions, and interrupting when Chris or Pat "break the rules.")

Therapist: You both did a good job of learning these new listening and speaking skills today. I know that we didn't actually solve the problem yet but at least you now know how to listen in a way that seems to work better for you. Next week we can pick up here and take it to the next step of problem solving and conflict resolution so that you can both feel good. Until then, how would you feel about practicing these speaking and listening skills at home this week?
Pat/Chris: OK.
Therapist: Let's review and write down the rules for speaker and listener so you'll remember. I'd suggest that you select an easy or light topic to practice with this week. Until you learn to do this more fluidly, it's probably best to save the really hot arguments for our sessions rather than at home. Is that OK with you?

(Pat and Chris agree and there is a brief discussion of when to do this homework assignment.)

In the preceding excerpt, the therapist uses the Cognitive Therapy principles of collaboration and discovery to help the couple understand the benefits of the new skills they are acquiring. Notice that the therapist uses questions to guide the couple toward reflecting on their experience and articulating in their own words the advantages of this communication style. By shaping the clients' discovery process in this manner, the therapist helps the couple to integrate skill acquisition and increases motivation to practice the skills learned. It is part of the philosophy of Cognitive Therapy to learn by analyzing one's own experience. This is preferable to learning that is based on either didactic lecture or unexamined experience.

COMMON DIFFICULTIES THAT IMPEDE COMMUNICATION SKILLS ACQUISITION

Teaching couples to listen to their partner's view is critical, especially since there is a natural tendency to interpret events in a self-serving way (Tyler & Devinitz, 1981). However, there are a number of factors that can impede a couple's ability to learn and practice new communication skills. Three common areas of difficulty are interpersonal deficits, intense affect, and interfering beliefs.

Interpersonal Deficits. Some individuals lack basic interpersonal skills even in nonconflict situations. One way to assess deficits in this area is to inquire whether either spouse has difficulty speaking or listening in their relationships with others and in everyday situations. Observing each spouse's ability to listen and talk with the therapist in session can also help assess possible problem areas.

These difficulties can range from organic learning disabilities (e.g., difficulty processing complex auditory input) to psycholearning difficulties such as a poor awareness of feelings or difficulty empathizing with others.

Additional assessment (e.g., neuropsychological testing) may be necessary to determine whether or not organic deficits are present. It will then be important to educate the couple regarding limitations posed by organic difficulties. The therapist and couple can then problem solve methods for communicating that assist the impaired member of the couple (e.g., writing out major points in discussion for visual processing).

If there are psycholearning deficits, several individual or conjoint sessions may be necessary in order to teach one or both partners the skills they lack. For example, adults who are not aware of or attuned to their feelings can be provided a list of feelings and can be assisted in identifying certain bodily sensations associated with each. Assignments to identify feelings from a list in situations where discomfort is experienced may help the individual develop a greater awareness of feelings in a brief period of time.

Intense Affect. Most couples have difficulty communicating clearly when they are extremely angry, anxious, or depressed. In fact, high affective arousal appears to be correlated with cognitive processing errors (Beck, Emery, et al., 1985; Beck, Rush, et al., 1979). If one or both partners are in a rage it is unrealistic to expect them to be able to complete a communication exercise easily.

Therefore, it is important to coach the couple in methods for reducing high affect before practicing new communication strategies. If one member of the couple is clinically anxious or depressed (even outside of the couple conflict), individual sessions may be helpful in alleviating the distress.

Anger is the most frequent intense emotion that may interfere with a couple's practice of communication skills. Although it is necessary for the couple to learn to talk in new ways about the things that make them angry, it is optimal to do this when their anger is at a low to moderate range of intensity. Therefore, couples should be instructed in methods of mutual "time out" when anger becomes so intense that communication of it is destructive rather than constructive for the relationship.

Beck (1988) describes the use of "color zones" to identify a couple's degree of anger and control. The blue zone describes a calm range of affect with good ability to communicate. The yellow zone describes a range of anger in which there is still control over thoughts, words, and actions. The red zone is marked by loss of control in words, sometimes physical attack, and also a high degree of distortion in thinking characterized by an extremely negative view of the partner.

Couples can be instructed to practice communication skills at first only when they are in the blue zone. As their skill increases, they can work constructively with each other in the yellow zone without the risk of escalating suddenly to the red zone. Since discussions in the red zone are characterized by attacks, it is

63

preferable that the couple stop discussions when the red zone is entered; either partner can call a "time out" at any point.

Time outs are usually brief (approximately 5 minutes; longer if necessary depending on the couple) and are intended to allow each person to cool down into a more constructive emotional zone. It is helpful to make time-out guidelines explicit in the therapy session. For example, the couple should discuss mutually acceptable places they each may go during the time-out period. For one couple, going into another room was sufficient, but actually leaving the house exacerbated the situation. For another couple, it might be desirable that one of the partners physically leave the home for awhile in order to reduce the risk of a physical attack.

Of course, if there is physical abuse in the relationship, personal safety from violence must be made a priority. In cases where there is a history of physical abuse by one or both partners, it may be necessary to effect a complete separation for a period of time until physical safety can be assured. There is a great deal of literature (Gangley, 1981; Neidig & Friedman, 1984; NiCarthy, 1982; Saunders, 1982; Sonkin & Durphy, 1982) on strategies to reduce physical violence between spouses. Therapists working with abusive spouses should familiarize themselves with the special dynamics of these cases and also community resources available to help the couple (e.g., shelters for victims of domestic violence, therapy groups for batterers).

Interfering Beliefs. Many couples have the potential to acquire good communication skills and yet often do not practice them even in moderate anger situations. Couples may sincerely want to improve their relationship yet display little effort. This can be puzzling to therapists and often is frustrating. Rather than viewing these occurrences as signs of "resistance," in Cognitive Therapy such circumstances can be viewed as signals that there are important thoughts and assumptions interfering with communication and change efforts.

Hopelessness is one of the most prevalent impediments to change. Common hopeless beliefs include: "My partner can't change," "It's too late for us," "Our problems are unsolvable," "We are too different to understand each other," "Things will only get worse if we talk about it," and "My efforts won't help anything."

Most couples hold some hopelessness beliefs at the beginning of therapy, so it is important for therapists to actively search for and identify hopeless beliefs in order to address these early in therapy. One way to identify and isolate these types of beliefs is to administer the *Beliefs About Change Questionnaire* (Beck, 1988) mentioned in Chapter 3 (p. 22) which assesses 14 areas of hopelessness and other attitudes that can slow the therapy if not addressed.

Once hopelessness has been identified, the therapist can assist in changing these beliefs by helping the couple test them. For example, if one person believes his or her partner is incapable of change, an experiment can be set up to test this belief. The following therapy excerpt illustrates this process.

Ann: I don't see the point. He says he'll change when he's here, but I know him. As soon as we leave here, he'll stop trying.

Therapist: That's an important idea to bring up, Ann. If what you say is true, how does that affect your willingness to try these things at home?

Ann: It seems like a joke to me. He's just going through the motions to say he tried and it's my fault.

Therapist: I would imagine that makes you not want to try to do things differently. You must feel somewhat hopeless.

Ann: Yes, I do. I feel defeated.

Therapist: Well, before we accept defeat, maybe we could test out this idea of yours. If Tony doesn't change, then we'll all have to figure out what that means and what to do about it. Yet if Tony does change, perhaps that would make you feel better about your marriage and about Tony?

Ann: Yes, I suppose so.

Therapist: We've been talking about your wish for Tony to treat you more lovingly. How will you know if he changes this week?

Ann: If he doesn't criticize me.

Therapist: Alright. How much does he criticize you now?

Ann: All the time.

Therapist: How many times a day?

Ann: Maybe 20 times.

Therapist: Twenty times. Now, he could change and improve on this and yet still criticize you. For instance, maybe criticize you 10 times a day.

Ann: That means he doesn't love me!

Therapist: Well, it certainly doesn't feel like love when we're criticized. Yet before we can rebuild love in your relationship we have to first find out if change is possible, right?

Ann: Yes.

Therapist: Have you ever tried to change a strong habit? For instance, as a computer programmer, have you ever switched to a different software package where commands were different from what was familiar before?

Ann: Sure.

Therapist: Did you change your habits 100%, immediately?

Ann: No. At first I made a lot of mistakes until I got used to the new system.

Therapist: OK. Whenever we make a change, even if we try hard we slip into old habits without thinking. But if we are trying to change, our mistakes get less and less over time. Do you see how Tony might need to have some time to change, and that even an improvement from 20 to 10 criticisms a day might signal real change?

Ann: I see what you mean. But each criticism hurts.

Therapist: That's important. So perhaps we need to do two things. First, you need to keep track of the number of criticisms Tony makes - to see if there is any reduction in the criticism. If you don't keep track, then even one instance of criticism might hurt so much you will decide he is not changing even when real change is occurring. Second, perhaps you should write down the criticisms so we can talk about them here and help you with your hurt and to find out if there is any pattern to the criticism so we can help Tony change even more.

Ann: OK. I'll give it a try.

Therapist: Tony, what do you think about the idea of Ann keeping track of your critical statements? Do you think this will help determine if you are changing this as you agreed to do?

Tony: Yes. I do try to change but when Annie jumps on me for slipping up, that makes me mad and then I get even more hot.

Therapist: So it would help you if Ann just counted and wrote them down instead of pointing them out to you each time.

Tony: Yeah. That would make it better.

Therapist: Well, we have a plan now that might help us learn about change in your relationship. We've already learned some things that might make change more possible. Ann, could you summarize what we've discussed about change so far?

Ann: It doesn't happen all at once. If I get mad at Tony for what he does, it makes him mad.

Therapist: Good summary. And I'm going to make a note for us to talk more about the hurt that you feel the next time that we meet. But before we leave today, I'd like to suggest that we discuss some ways that you can each be more loving to each other during the week in a positive fashion . . . .

This case excerpt illustrates the use of "Socratic questioning" (Beck, Emery, et al., 1985) to help Ann understand how her definition of change might be contributing to her hopelessness. Socratic questioning is a type of inductive questioning used to guide the client in examining and testing out beliefs. Rather than the therapist arguing directly with Ann's ideas, the therapist asked questions to help Ann relate Tony's change attempts to her own prior efforts at making changes. By asking Ann to compare her own experience to Tony's in a step-by-step fashion, the therapist helped weaken her original biased belief that only complete change was noteworthy. Finally, an experiment was devised to evaluate Ann's idea that Tony would not change rather than discounting her hopelessness or simply "reassuring" her.

Note that the content, context, and meaning of Tony's criticism were put off until the next session because the therapist decided Ann's hopelessness would interfere with the probability she would notice any change that Tony made in this early stage of therapy. At the same time, the therapist acknowledged the importance of Ann's feelings and assured her that these issues would be addressed in the next session.

Similarly, brief experiments can test other hopeless beliefs such as whether talking about things (in the therapy session) makes the tension worse. As in the preceding case example, the therapist works to help the couple evaluate change efforts in a realistic way so that progress made is not discounted based on imperfection or only partial success.

A second type of belief that can sidetrack good communication concerns intolerance of emotional discomfort in others.

Many people hold beliefs such as, "I'm bad if I cause someone else pain," or "If my partner feels pain, then I must fix it." These beliefs can make couples unwilling to express hurt and anger or can lead the listening partner to quickly problem solve or prematurely apologize rather than empathically hear and understand their partner's feelings.

These beliefs can be tested out through the use of thought records as described in Chapter 3. The therapist can also help the couple evaluate the advantages and disadvantages of these beliefs. As with most beliefs, true change is unlikely to occur until the couple are helped to "try on" new behaviors (in this case, expressing or listening to painful feelings) and then to evaluate the costs and benefits of this new approach.

In many cases, this avoidance of emotional discomfort is related to childhood experiences with dysfunctional patterns of emotional expression in the family of origin. In these cases, it is often helpful to review with the couple the early patterns that contributed particularly to these beliefs. Once clients understand how these patterns developed, they can more clearly evaluate whether or not the pattern is functional in their current relationship. Of course, if the current partner does support dysfunctional patterns, both must be helped to change.

A third type of belief that can interfere with communication efforts involves fear of intimacy. Such thoughts include: "If they get to know me, they'll reject me," "If I express my true feelings, I'll be humiliated," "I'm better off on my own," "It's risky to talk about emotions - things can get out of hand," or "If I let myself get close and it doesn't work out, I won't be able to handle the pain."

Again, fear of intimacy beliefs are important to identify so the therapist can help the client evaluate their usefulness and accuracy. Once identified, these beliefs can be tested against the client's experience. These beliefs lend themselves well to the use of a continuum.

For example, the belief "I'll be better off on my own" is expressed as an absolute. The therapist can draw a continuum on a piece of paper with the endpoints labeled "0% On My Own" and "100% On My Own." Different areas of the relationship can be identified in which the individual functions at different points along the continuum. For example, one individual might make a decision about buying a house "0% on my own," where to go on vacation "35% on my own," and decide about a job "98% on my own."

The continuum can help illustrate to the individual that there are advantages to both being "on your own" and having a partner. The couple can then discuss the risks and benefits of mutual involvement in different areas of their life. Many fear of intimacy beliefs can be modified by helping the client discover that intimacy is not an all-or-none proposition.

Although this section outlines three major areas of belief that can interfere with good communication, there are dozens of other types of beliefs and thousands of idiosyncratic beliefs that could interfere. It is important for therapists to actively search for these beliefs (e.g., by asking about automatic thoughts that occur during the communication training exercise) so they can be evaluated directly in the therapy. It is also important to ask about images or memories that occur (e.g., "He seems like an elephant to me, unmovable") because these can be very powerful and can also be changed through cognitive methods (cf. Edwards, 1989).

PROBLEM SOLVING

Learning to talk and listen well are the fundamental building blocks of good communication. Once the couple have mastered these, they are ready to learn problem resolution strategies for those areas in which they disagree.

The ability to hear and summarize the partner's viewpoint is a good starting point for problem solving. The couple can be instructed to write down each person's main points before starting to problem solve. Ideally solutions will be sought that meet at least some of both partners' needs and expectations.

Jacobson and Margolin (1979), developed a problem-solving manual for couples that outlines strategies for constructive conflict resolution. In this manual they describe a number of principles for successful problem solving, including: setting an agenda, positively and specifically defining problems, discussing only one problem at a time, focusing on solutions instead of blame, and mutual compromise.

These principles are similar to those used in Cognitive Therapy with Couples. Once the couple are able to talk and listen as described previously, these skills can be employed to set an agenda for problem solving. Each problem can be specifically defined - such as division of child care responsibilities.

Then, one simple approach to problem resolution is for the couple to brainstorm all possible solutions and choose one agreeable to both. The couple should be encouraged by the therapist to generate as many solutions as possible, even if some seem far-fetched. For example, six solutions might be generated to handle Saturday child care. The first four might be agreeable to Martha and solutions four, five, and six agreeable to Mick. Since the fourth solution is agreeable to both, this one would be chosen.

Although this simple problem-solving approach can successfully resolve many couple disagreements, it is not always ideal. In some cases, a problem may be of greater significance to one partner than the other. In this instance, it makes sense to choose a solution which is satisfactory to the most concerned partner, even if this solution is not preferred by both.

Sometimes there is no mutually satisfactory solution. In this case, couples need to decide who will be satisfied in the current instance with perhaps a tradeoff later; for example, "I'll get my way this time, you get your way next time." Alternatively, some couples may decide to each be partially satisfied (e.g., "I'll watch the kids in the morning, and you watch them in the afternoon"). Other couples may prefer to have neither party satisfied (e.g., "I won't go to my reunion, and you won't go skiing; we'll both stay home with the kids").

In the most flexible of couples, each of these types of solutions will be practiced some of the time. In couples therapy it is helpful to explore all of these problem-solving alternatives so that couples feel less stuck when they do disagree.

During this problem-solving phase of therapy, a number of hidden issues frequently emerge. These involve both systems issues such as dynamics of power in the relationship and beliefs that may interfere with successful problem solving. The following sections outline strategies for helping the couple overcome these types of roadblocks.

Power Differences in the Relationship. In this book "power" refers to the ability to influence one's partner. Almost all relationships have some power differences. For some couples, the power differentials may be divided - for instance, one partner may have more authority to make decisions about money whereas another may have more say in how time is spent. Other couples may strive to divide all decisions equally and yet differences in knowledge, finances, or status may subtly influence decision making in the couple.

The problem-resolution strategies used in Cognitive Therapy are based on a collaborative model of equal power. In addition to the therapy's humanistic philosophical roots, the commitment to shared decision making is grounded in research that suggests (a) dissatisfied couples are more likely to use coercion rather than reciprocity to influence each other (Stuart, 1969), and (b) coercive influence strategies are less effective than positive methods of influence (Raven, Centers, & Rodrigues, 1975).

A therapist needs to recognize when a couple are not going to easily adapt such a reciprocity model for their relationship. In these cases, additional work needs to be done with the couple to help prepare them for problem-resolution strategies.

For instance, some couples are established within a rigid, hierarchical system. In these couples, one person has the designated final word ("I will say what is best for the family.") This "absolute rule" mentality is not limited to gender roles. Sometimes it is the wealthy partner or the more "attractive" partner who has all the decision power.

In order to help create a collaborative set in a couple with extreme or rigid power differences, the therapist needs to help the couple realize that it is to their mutual advantage to share decision making. One way to accomplish this goal is to ask the couple about the advantages and disadvantages of their current decision-making style, emphasizing the relative merits of using both partners' knowledge and strengths to solve problems.

Power differences in some couples result from the unexamined continuation of cultural values with which they were raised (e.g., both may have been raised in families where the wife held all the responsibility and decision-making power for child-rearing, and the husband had all of the responsibility for financial decisions). In these cases, the therapist can ask questions to help the couple identify areas in their life where they have already broken tradition to their benefit (e.g., the wife may be working outside the home whereas her mother would never have considered doing this). Then, the couple and therapist can examine together whether following tradition in decision-making patterns is to their mutual benefit or detriment.

If one or both members of a couple rigidly adhere to a system of unilateral power, the therapist needs to consider whether couples therapy can be effective (if problem resolution is an area of concern). Alternatives would be individual therapy (to help each individual examine his or her options in or outside of this relationship) or helping the couple adjust to the status quo in their relationship. The latter course is usually chosen only if the relationship is nonabusive and mutually acceptable. For example, a very dependent person may choose to stay with a very domineering partner for security and be unwilling to explore other options in therapy.

Styles of Influence in Relationships. Power is as much a cognitive construct as a behavioral one. Sometimes a strongly influential partner will perceive himself or herself as powerless and therefore not take any responsibility for the problems in the relationship. By examining different styles of power expression, couples can see that each exerts influence over the other in both effective and ineffective ways.

Some people use direct influence methods of persuasion. Direct persuasion can be accomplished through discussions or may consist of persistent nagging until the partner complies with a request. These direct methods can be perceived as positive or negative depending upon tone. For example, a discussion can be an angry interchange, a threatening demand, or a reciprocal exchange of ideas. Even nagging, which is usually negatively reinforcing, could be positively received if done with tact and humor.

Others use more indirect methods of influence. A woman might leave out a copy of *Love Is Never Enough* (Beck, 1988) hoping her partner will see it, read it, and understand that the relationship needs to be changed. A man might describe the dinner options, emphasizing the delicious qualities of his first choice and yet ask his wife to choose the restaurant.

Influence strategies can be evaluated in terms of whether or not they accomplish the couple's goals while minimizing negative side effects and maximizing positive side effects. The couple is encouraged to weigh the advantages and disadvantages of different methods.

For example, nagging and a written reminder note may both result in action by a partner; yet the written note may minimize friction and irritation within the couple and therefore be a more desirable method of influence. Some methods of influence (e.g., a discussion in which both partners disclose their feelings and reasons for a decision) can constructively deepen the relationship and would be preferable to purely coercive methods.

Beliefs That Can Sidetrack Problem Solving. There are several common beliefs that can block even the best therapeutic attempts to teach couples problem-solving strategies. Often one partner will strongly hold the view, "I've already compromised too much," and be unwilling to negotiate. Beliefs about change can also impede problem solving. These beliefs include: "A little change is not enough," "We have to change too much," and "The solution needs to be perfect."

A person who believes he or she has already compromised too much perceives any negotiation as unfair. Therefore, the therapist must help this individual see some advantage to continued exchange in the relationship before problem solving can occur. A first step can be testing the client's perception to see if, in fact, this client has compromised to a much greater degree than the partner. Sometimes people are not aware of some of the compromises made by partners. A review of this history can also help the couple feel understood by the therapist.

Second, the advantages and disadvantages of clinging to a belief in "equal compromise" can be explored. Many intimate relationships do not require equality in compromise - for example, parent/child relationships are usually imbalanced, with the parent giving more than the child. Adult friendships are often imbalanced for periods of time depending upon needs and resources. It can be helpful to explore the reasons why adults are often willing to compromise more than half the time to make a relationship work.

However, if there has been a great imbalance in partner giving over a long period of time, there may need to be some acknowledgement of this in future problem solving. For example, the couple may agree that their goal for awhile will be to search for mutually acceptable solutions only rather than considering solutions solely preferred by the previously dominant partner. The therapist can emphasize that this is a temporary plan to restore goodwill and trust in the relationship.

If both partners agree there has been an imbalance in giving, it may also be desirable to have some symbolic redress made to the partner who feels drained by the relationship. One example would be a couple in which the husband agreed to do more than his share of the child care for a year so his wife could attend school.

If a couple have been in distress for a long period of time, they may feel that a little change will not be enough. Other couples fear that so much change will be required to improve their relationship that it is impossible to accomplish. One helpful approach for addressing these beliefs is to present a model of change to couples in which the goal of therapy is to make the smallest changes necessary to accomplish the largest positive effect.

A metaphor that illustrates this idea is that of the trajectory of a thrown object. A small shift in the angle of throw can make a large difference in how the object is received some distance away. With regard to couples, if one spouse makes a small change in behavior, this can be perceived as a major change by the partner because of the symbolic meaning of the behavior (K. A. Mooney, personal communication, August 22, 1989).

This idea can be tied to the broader cognitive model to include small changes in thinking, behavior, mood, and environment. As a collective, several very small changes can lead to profound shifts in the relationship.

Finally, some clients have difficulty solving problems because they are searching for perfect solutions. Examining the advantages and disadvantages of inaction versus imperfect action can often help these people loosen their perfectionistic standards. It is also helpful to identify and test the beliefs supporting the perfectionistic standards. Common beliefs accompanying perfectionism include: "Something terrible will happen if I don't do the best thing," "Inadequate solutions prove I/we am/are inadequate," and "Other people could figure out a better solution."

5.

THE STRUCTURE OF COGNITIVE THERAPY WITH COUPLES

COURSE AND FREQUENCY OF THERAPY SESSIONS

Although treatment length and the course of therapy vary according to the couple's problems and strengths, it is possible to specify stages of therapy completed for most couples in Cognitive Therapy.

Table 1 (pp. 76-77) outlines these stages and summarizes their rationale or methods. For each stage, one or more chapters in this book are listed which include information on the procedures and techniques helpful for its accomplishment. Although this table accurately describes the course of treatment for many couples, the order and length of time necessary to accomplish each stage depend upon the couple's needs and skills. Some stages may be emphasized several times during treatment.

Generally, couples therapy sessions are scheduled once a week for a 50-minute hour. If the couple are in crisis, two sessions per week may be helpful. Some therapists prefer 75-minute sessions to allow greater time to process the couple's information, especially early in the course of therapy when there is a high need for both assessment and treatment time.

As mentioned earlier, Cognitive Therapy is usually short term with a typical treatment length of 12 to 20 sessions. Of course, long-standing difficulties or problems complicated by a personality disorder in one or more members of the couple may lead to a

---

TABLE 1: COGNITIVE THERAPY WITH COUPLES:
STAGES OF TREATMENT

---

1. History and conceptualization of the couple's problems (Chapters 3 and 4)

   -- Gather assessment information
   -- Explain the treatment model in terms of the couple's history

2. Anger management (Chapter 4)

   -- At this stage, simply cooling down and containment of negatives

3. Increasing positive behaviors in the relationship (Chapter 4)

   -- Restores a positive foundation to the relationship
   -- Helps set up a positive expectation for change
   -- Introduces a collaborative set to the couple's at-home interactions

4. Teaching the couple to identify, test, and respond to key automatic thoughts (Chapter 4)

   -- Teach identification of automatic thoughts (AT's)
   -- Assign homework to write down AT's during problems
   -- Teach couple to evaluate and test out their AT's - in session, at home

5. Teaching communication skills (Chapter 4)

   -- Use standard techniques
   -- Combine with couple's awareness of AT's which interfere with effective speaking and listening; evaluate and test these AT's

6. Exploration of anger issues (Chapters 4 and 6)

   -- At surface level, learn to evaluate AT's associated with anger
   -- At deeper level, identify secret doubts, hurts, and hidden fears that fuel recurrent anger situations
   -- Help individuals and couple respond to these doubts, hurts, and fears, so perceived threats can be resolved more constructively

TABLE 1 (Continued)

7. Teaching problem-resolution strategies (Chapter 4)

    -- Use standard techniques
    -- Identify and test beliefs that interfere with standard methods

8. Identifying and changing dysfunctional attitudes and core assumptions (Chapter 6)

    -- Important for individuals and couples with rigid belief systems
    -- A key focus of cognitive therapy with personality disorders
    -- Examine the historical roots of core dysfunctional beliefs
    -- Test the current day validity/utility of these beliefs
    -- Help construct more adaptive attitudes through carefully designed behavioral experiments, prediction logs, and new experience logs

9. Relapse prevention (Chapter 5)

    -- Review principles and problem-solving strategies learned
    -- Anticipate future problems and brainstorm solutions
    -- Schedule a "check-up" appointment after termination

---

longer treatment course. Some additional treatment considerations for these cases are discussed in Chapter 6.

INDIVIDUAL VERSUS CONJOINT SESSIONS

Cognitive therapists meet with couples in both conjoint and individual sessions. Generally, most sessions will involve the couple together. It is often helpful, however, to meet with each person individually early in treatment to identify important individual issues that may not come out in the conjoint sessions. Individual sessions can also be helpful to explore some early family-of-origin issues which may be impacting the current relationship.

Usually, both members of the couple will be seen about the same number of times individually. This may be only once or for several sessions. If extensive individual therapy is required, it may be desirable for this to be done by a separate therapist.

As is apparent from the case dialogues excerpted in this book, cognitive therapists also work with individuals in the conjoint sessions. It can be therapeutic for a client to listen to a therapist discussing a problem, identifying and testing automatic thoughts, and empathizing with the feelings of his or her partner. Sometimes the distance provided by this secondary listening role allows a client to hear important feelings and ideas more clearly than in the past.

The issue of confidentiality must be addressed if the therapist is meeting with the couple both together and in individual sessions. Some therapists inform couples that any information given in the individual sessions will not be held in confidence from the partner; that is, information given in the individual sessions will be discussed openly in the conjoint sessions. This, of course, remains at the discretion of the therapist.

For several reasons, it may be better to have the individual sessions be fully confidential. Confidential individual sessions allow each member of the couple to disclose information to the therapist that may have importance for the couple's therapy but which the individual does not yet feel ready to disclose to his or her partner. For example, one partner may have been a victim of incest, never having revealed the impact that this had within the current relationship. A spouse may be having an affair and not feel ready to reveal this (see Chapter 6).

If the individual sessions are confidential, the therapist can work on these individual issues impacting the couple. The therapist can protect individual confidentiality and also help the couple by exploring with each spouse separately the pros and cons of discussing the hidden issues within the couple's sessions. If an individual has important issues that he or she is not willing to discuss in the couple's sessions, the therapist can encourage individual work on these issues either to resolve them or to lead to greater willingness to explore them in the couple's sessions.

Working with the client's automatic thoughts about the meaning of hidden issues can be very helpful. For example, sometimes people do not share important information with their partners because they believe that it will hurt their partner or cause distress in the relationship. It is helpful to test out these ideas because often hidden information leads to greater distance in the relationship than would be caused by its revelation and discussion. Sometimes people have a belief that it is unfair to cause their partner pain. This type of belief can be evaluated as described in Chapter 4 (pp. 50-54). Chapter 6 describes the utility of evaluating the meaning of affairs.

✝ SETTING AGENDAS

One of the structural aspects of Cognitive Therapy that can help therapist and couple stay on track and work collaboratively is setting an agenda at the beginning of each session. Agendas can be set very conversationally by simply saying, "My plan for today was to review what you learned this week, discuss areas in which you feel 'stuck,' and continue practicing the methods we rehearsed last week. Are there additional or different things you wanted to make sure we accomplished today?" Alternatively, the therapist could start by asking, "What did you want to discuss today" and then add review of homework and other topics carried over from the last session, asking the couple if these are relevant for this session. Discussion of previous homework should always be on the agenda.

Some therapists not familiar with Cognitive Therapy might think setting an agenda is controlling on the part of the therapist. In reality, agenda setting usually serves to put the client more in control. Without an agenda, clients often start talking about topics that feel safer, leaving other critical topics for later in the session. Because the therapist may not know these other topics exist, he or she may explore the initial topics in such depth that there is no time remaining for the other topics important to the couple.

By setting an agenda, therapist and clients can collaboratively prioritize which issues to discuss in that session. Part of structuring the therapy can also involve deciding how much time to spend on each topic so the discussion is problem oriented and not rambling. Of course, agendas, once set, need to be flexible. Sometimes a topic assigned 15 minutes of session time may open up core areas of difficulty. The agenda may then need to be adjusted or changed entirely to respond to the emotional and cognitive information revealed.

⚐ HOMEWORK ASSIGNMENTS

Part of Cognitive Therapy involves home practice and learning assignments. Research on Cognitive Therapy with depression showed that clients who did homework learning tasks showed greater and faster improvement than those who did not do homework (Persons, Burns, & Perloff, 1988; Primakoff, Epstein, & Covi, 1986). The rationale for assigning homework is that people learn best by doing. Since the cognitive model links thoughts, feelings, behavior, biology, and environment, homework tasks can be assigned that facilitate small changes in one or more of these areas to discover what larger changes result from these small adjustments.

There are two basic types of homework assignments in Cognitive Therapy: observational and experimental. These assignments may be given individually or to the couple and may involve thoughts, feelings, behavior, biology, or environment. Whatever the assignment, it should be collaboratively designed to be relevant to the couple's central concerns, something the clients have the skill to accomplish, and, ideally, begun in the therapy session. These latter characteristics will help increase the likelihood of homework compliance.

Observational assignments include: noticing and writing down feelings and automatic thoughts, keeping track of positive or problem behaviors, observing other couples to notice similarities or differences in behavior or speaking patterns, and keeping a timed journal to see if patterns exist and if they are tied to times of the day, activity, or mood.

Experimental learning tasks are as varied as couples' problems. These include assignments such as: trying out a new behavior or communication style and recording the outcome, completing an automatic thought record and seeing whether this reduces a distressing emotion, changing the time of day or conditions (e.g., alcohol intake) under which a certain interaction occurs, and asking the couple to try out new problem-solving strategies such as "post-it" notes instead of nagging.

These homework tasks are critical for achieving the goals of changing beliefs or building new skills. It is important for the therapist and clients to be aware that it may require continued practice or experimentation over a period of time before reliable change is achieved. For example, a husband practiced listening to his wife without interrupting or prematurely problem solving. These experiments went well and she felt as if he was hearing her better. However, she was unwilling to be convinced this problem was solved until she and he were able to maintain this pattern over a period of several months.

Sometimes clients do not complete the homework assigned. There are many reasons for homework noncompliance including both therapist and client factors. Therapists can contribute to homework noncompliance by: assigning too much homework, not choosing homework relevant to the couple's primary concerns, not asking about the homework in the next session, assigning homework that is beyond the skill level of the client, not describing the homework clearly, not asking the client to write down the homework, or neglecting to assess and problem solve ahead of time the reasons the client may not do the homework.

Even if the homework is well chosen and integrated with the therapy, clients may still not complete it. In these cases, it is important that therapist and clients understand what is preventing homework completion. Sometimes, pragmatic problems interfere (e.g., the client was ill, or the time set aside for homework was interrupted by an emergency). In other cases, clients may not do the homework because they think their problem is hopeless (see case excerpt in Chapter 4, pp. 65-67).

Other beliefs the client may hold that can lead to homework noncompliance are: "I can't make change happen," "This is how I am and I can't change," "The only thing that will work is _____. This homework is meaningless," and "If we try this assignment, it will make things worse." The therapist can be alert for these types of beliefs and test them through Socratic questioning in the session and also through assigning small homework steps as a test of these beliefs.

℣ FOLLOW-UP BOOSTER SESSIONS

Relapse prevention has been a major focus of research and clinical practice in the last decade (Marlatt & Gordon, 1985). Because it provides structured learning, Cognitive Therapy is ideally suited to help prevent relapse. In the final therapy sessions the therapist and couple can review the strategies learned and problem-solve steps for handling future difficulties. The therapist can give the couple a variety of problem scenarios similar to the ones handled in therapy and ask them to demonstrate how they would manage these on their own.

An additional step to help maintain treatment gains is to schedule follow-up booster sessions. The couple can be invited to make one or more appointments in the 6 months following the end of regularly scheduled therapy. These sessions are helpful even if the couple continue to do well post-therapy. The couple can review what skills and patterns are maintaining their relationship success. The booster sessions can also be used to answer questions and solve problems the couple may not have adequately resolved themselves.

6.
SPECIAL ISSUES IN COUPLES THERAPY

A number of special circumstances occur frequently enough in couples therapy to warrant special discussion. Eight important issues will be discussed in this chapter: (a) crisis situations, (b) anger and violence, (c) infidelity, (d) when one wants out and the other doesn't, (e) when is it time to end the relationship, (f) how to modify the therapy when there are other psychiatric disorders within the couple (e.g., personality disorders), (g) cultural issues, and (h) therapy with gay and lesbian couples.

CRISIS SITUATIONS

Often a crisis will lead a couple to begin therapy, even if they normally would not consider treatment. In some of these cases the couple will decide to seek help on the advice of a member of the clergy or a family member.

Crisis situations can involve circumstances such as unwanted pregnancies, the discovery of infidelity, an argument resulting in a physical fight or an arrest, drug or alcohol abuse, and so forth. Crises such as these usually warrant emergency intervention, sometimes over several sessions. Diffusing the emergency typically takes precedence over the normal course of intake. Once volatility is reduced, the therapist can proceed with more global assessment and treatment goals following the intake procedure described in Chapter 3.

When working with crisis situations, the following steps may be helpful to structure the sessions:

Cognitive Therapy With Couples

Step 1. Quickly conceptualize the couple's immediate problem. This session should be an extended visit and used to assess immediate problems and resources. The therapist may also need to assess whether or not the couple can safely reside together during the crisis. The use of questionnaires/inventories at this juncture is usually not feasible.

Step 2. Immediately teach the couple to monitor their feeling level and, if possible, to identify automatic thoughts contributing to their distress. This instruction should be paired with teaching the couple how to call time out and/or separate during arguments or periods of agitation.

Step 3. Explore alternative responses and behaviors. If a behavior is removed, it should be replaced with an alternative behavior (e.g., replace yelling with writing out disagreements). If the couple decide to separate, ask them to decide where to go until they can safely reconvene.

Step 4. Practice Steps 1 through 3 in the office and ask them to agree to use these steps as a defusing procedure. Attaining a collaborative set at this point is extremely important (see Chapter 2, p. 16).

Step 5. Schedule a follow-up session as soon as possible. It may be desirable to have telephone contact between the emergency visit and the follow-up session.

Step 6. The therapist must use clinical judgment to recommend whether or not the couple should live together during the crisis. This is especially important if the crisis involves an issue of physical abuse. The therapist is urged to proceed with caution with such cases and may want to consider temporary alternative living arrangements. The use of basic problem-solving techniques should be applied with modification for short-term use (see Chapter 4, pp. 69-74).

ANGER AND VIOLENCE SITUATIONS

Throughout this book, case examples have emphasized anger and conflict situations because these are the most typical expressions of relationship problems. For some couples, however, these problems escalate to a dangerous level with the presence or risk of physical violence. Some couples may make frequent crisis phone calls to the therapist, perhaps questioning if they should separate because the anger is so intense.

When anger is at high levels, additional care is required on the part of the therapist. If violence is a risk, personal safety for both members of the couple must take priority over other therapy goals. Sometimes physical separation is the only assurance of safety in the couple and should be very strongly recommended.

One woman called her therapist and reported that her husband had hit her and threatened to kill her during an argument the night before. The therapist helped her explore options for safety including living temporarily with her sister or calling a local shelter for abused women. Furthermore, the therapist suggested she not meet with her husband alone but rather talk with him either on the phone or with other people present until the crisis was resolved. It is also usually advisable in cases of physical violence that the abused partner be encouraged to file a police report.

Therapists not familiar with domestic violence are encouraged to educate themselves about the special dynamics of relationship violence (Finkelhor et al., 1983; Gelles, 1972; Pagelow, 1981; Walker, 1979, 1984) and about local community resources such as groups and shelters for victims of domestic violence and therapy groups for batterers.

A Cognitive Therapy perspective is helpful for work with violent couples. A number of common beliefs can be identified and tested using the cognitive model. For example, a batterer might say, "It's not my fault! When she acts that way I get so mad I can't help but to hit her." The therapist can help him see he does have choice and control over his response. Good Socratic questions include, "What have you done when you get furious with someone at work or with me (in therapy)" or "What would you do if you became that angry and a police officer was standing next to you?"

People who are battered in relationships also have beliefs that keep them in the violent cycle. Common beliefs include: "This will never happen again," "I can't make it on my own so I have no choice but to endure this," "I did something to deserve this," "We're married so I have to put up with this," or "They were drunk so this isn't really a serious problem."

For couples with a high degree of violence risk, it is recommended that both receive individual counseling to help them test these types of beliefs and learn strategies to reduce the risk of violence. Often, the couple may need to live separately until both are out of crisis enough to work on their mutual problems in the same household without risk. Group therapy with other batterers or victims of violence can be very helpful (NiCarthy, Merriam, & Coffman, 1984; Sonkin & Durphy, 1982).

Even in couples without physical violence, intense anger can be extremely distressing. The cognitive model of anger as outlined by Beck (1988) can help couples identify the root causes of their discord. Beck suggests that hurt and fear lie beneath most anger responses. The therapist can help each member of the couple identify the hurt and fear beneath their anger by asking questions such as, "What makes you angry about that," "What does this mean to you," "What does this say about you," or "What's the worst that could happen if this continues?" By asking these questions repeatedly and teaching the couple to do this with themselves when angry, they can learn to identify hurt and fear whenever anger is present.

The advantage of looking for the hurt and fear attached to the anger is twofold. First, these feelings fuel the anger cycle which may not be fully resolved unless there is an expression of and response to these additional emotions. Second, it is normal for people to respond to anger in their partner with defensiveness or anger themselves. Expressions of hurt or fear are usually met with apology or reassurance. Therefore, if couples can learn to express the hurt and fear behind their anger, there is a good chance that conflict can be replaced by mutual listening, support, and problem solving.

INFIDELITY

Affairs often accompany or precede relationship distress. Issues regarding confidentiality when an affair is revealed in an individual session were discussed in Chapter 5. This chapter explores the meaning of affairs and how a therapist can help clients consider the implications an affair has for the primary relationship.

Some couples and therapists believe that once there is an affair the relationship is doomed. This need not be the case, although sometimes an affair does signal the end of a relationship. The important task for a therapist when an affair is revealed is to discover the meaning this other relationship has for the individual having the affair and for the primary relationship.

One client had a series of affairs because he believed this was normal behavior for a man. His father had always had a mistress and talked with him as he grew up about the importance of keeping a sexual partner in addition to one's wife. This man truly loved his wife and could not understand why she was upset with his affairs, because none of these women were significant loves for him. These beliefs were discussed in the couple's therapy, and he was able to see that his affairs were damaging his relationship with his wife. He was willing to abandon the affairs and test the idea that it was possible for a man to be sexually satisfied with one woman.

One common reason people have affairs is that they are dissatisfied with their current relationship and feel the chances for change are hopeless. In these cases, the person having the affair is often willing to terminate the affair once they see that their primary relationship is improving.

Another common belief supporting affairs is, "If I am feeling this attraction to X, then I have to act on this attraction." The therapist can intervene with this belief by using Socratic questions which will help the individual discover that many times in life he or she has not acted on intense attractions. People experience romantic attractions to movie stars, teachers, employers, married colleagues, therapists, and others, and they may not choose to pursue these attractions. Identifying these types of relationships in the client's life will help him or her realize that attraction does not necessitate action.

Sometimes people have affairs because they "fall in love" with someone else. These affairs can be the most difficult to resolve, especially if the person having the affair feels committed to both people. The person in love with two people needs either to choose one of them or try to work out an agreement with all involved that he or she engage in two relationships. Very few couples tolerate the stress involved in agreed-upon nonmonogamous relationships, although this is an option some couples may choose to explore.

When a person is in love with someone other than the primary partner, he or she may also choose to end the current relationship in order to pursue the new relationship. In these cases, the couple's therapist can help them separate. In addition, the therapist can help the couple by making sure the individual having the affair considers this decision carefully.

For example, the affair may represent avoidance of some developmental challenge for the individual. One woman wanted to leave her husband of 10 years because "the romance was gone." After several individual sessions she realized she had never dealt with long-term relationship issues before and the intimacy struggles with her husband frightened her. In addition, there were many positive qualities about her marriage she was not appreciating. When she considered that these same relationship problems would probably appear in the new relationship in 10 years she decided to remain with her husband because he was more the type of man she believed would love her and help her work through these struggles.

Therapists are often asked to advise whether or not the partner should be told about an affair that has been secret. This decision must be made by the person who has had the affair, but the following issues can be considered: What did the affair mean? How will the relationship be helped/hurt if the affair is revealed? How will the relationship be helped/hurt if the affair is concealed? What steps can be taken to re-establish trust in the relationship? If the decision is made to talk about the affair, the therapist can help the individual tell the partner and also support a developmental process of adjusting to this potential crisis in the relationship. In addition, therapist and client can discuss whether or not the partner should be informed of the affair during a therapy session or in a more private setting.

Finally, until the AIDS epidemic is stopped, important ethical questions are posed for therapists working with clients who are having affairs in secret. Professional therapy organizations have not made formal decisions on a therapist's obligations, although some guidelines can be suggested.

At a minimum, therapists should discuss AIDS and safe sexual practices with clients having sex with multiple partners. If a therapist believes a client is not using safe sex, there may be grounds to break confidentiality to warn their sexual partners.

Ideally, therapists will work with clients to encourage them to use safe sex and to responsibly inform their partners of any risky practices. Cognitive therapists can help clients test any beliefs that may interfere with these responsible practices.

Therapists are encouraged to consult the ethics committees of their professional associations for guidance on ethical management of particular cases.

WHEN ONE WANTS OUT
AND THE OTHER DOESN'T

Frequently one partner wants to end a relationship and the other does not. The therapist can work with the individual who wishes to end the relationship in order to understand his or her reasons and to test potential distorted beliefs such as hopelessness about the potential for improvement in the relationship. If the decision is made to end the relationship, then special therapeutic strategies can be used to help each person adapt to this decision.

The person who is being left may have pragmatic fears about issues such as finances and child custody arrangements which the therapist can help problem solve. In addition, often, when a relationship ends, beliefs are triggered that can make the separation process more difficult. Cognitive Therapy is ideally suited to help test these beliefs.

One type of thought triggered by the end of a relationship involves dependency beliefs such as: "I can't make it without this person." As with all grief reactions, the cognitive therapist will empathize with the sadness and loss first. Then the therapist can help by gently testing this belief. One strategy is to ask about the times before and during this relationship when this person did cope well independently of his or her partner. It can also be helpful to review other supports and important relationships to help the person see that he or she is not totally alone.

Another common belief is, "Something must be wrong with me." In order to test this assumption, the therapist can ask the client to recall other people whom he or she respects and likes and who have been left by a partner. The therapist asks, "Was something wrong with them? Why do you suppose a partner left them if they are good people? Could any of these reasons apply to your situation?" Another strategy is to review several people this person cares for but would not choose for a close romantic relationship. Exploring the reasons the client would not select these good people as mates can be a helpful reminder that relationships do not last simply because people are "good enough."

Partners who are leaving the relationship may also have beliefs that make the separation process damaging for them. One common reaction is guilt for causing their partner so much pain. It can be helpful for some clients to examine and learn from the process of leaving the relationship. Is there some behavior or attitude that it might be helpful for them to change?

Often, however, the discomfort in the person leaving the relationship is supported by an accompanying belief: "I'm responsible for the pain. I must make the pain go away." It can be helpful to review with these clients the reasons they are leaving the relationship. Usually these reasons are ones for which the couple share the responsibility, rather than being the result of one person's actions.

Also, it can be helpful to discuss the pain they have undergone in deciding to leave and consider whether or not this pain has been useful. Most clients asked to evaluate the benefits of emotional pain understand that painful experiences are not 100% negative. Reviewing these experiences can help clients realize that their partners have a right to experience pain and learn from it as well.

Helping both members of a couple examine these and other attitudes prompted by the end of a relationship can increase the likelihood they will be able to talk directly with each other about the issues and problems still requiring resolution. In this way, individual and couples therapy can help relationships end as well as continue.

WHEN IS IT TIME TO
END THE RELATIONSHIP?

The preceding section prompts the question, "How does a therapist know when a relationship should end?" To paraphrase Jacqueline Persons (1989), "How do you know if your work with a couple is going poorly because it is a relationship failure or because it is a slow relationship success?"

The answer to this question is complex. First, the therapist should not decide that a relationship is poor based solely on the information provided by the couple at the beginning of therapy. Couples often begin therapy in a high degree of distress accompanied by hopelessness and perceptions of the relationship filtered through negative attitudes. It is axiomatic that when the initial distress bringing the couple to therapy is relieved, the couple will present a more positive picture of their life together.

The decision of whether to end a relationship is one that the couple should make. Often the relationship will improve somewhat and then worsen as troubling conflicts surface. A therapist's ability to conceptualize the origins of these problems can help expedite the therapy through these potential "stuck points." Persons' (1989) book on case formulation provides a useful guide for using a cognitive case conceptualization to understand and solve these therapeutic challenges.

In general, couples benefit from therapy if the therapist takes a hopeful and problem-solving stance throughout the couple's difficulties. As with depressed clients whose beliefs may be consistently negative and hopeless until the depression lifts, couples can sincerely believe their problems are unsolvable until they are successfully resolved. The therapist, then, often needs to provide the hope that problems, once defined, can be solved.

One therapist sought supervision for her work with a couple whose relationship had not improved over a 6-month period of therapy. The therapist felt hopeless and uncertain how to proceed with the couple. The supervisor was able to help her conceptualize the main beliefs for both husband and wife that appeared to be interfering with treatment progress. Once the therapist identified these beliefs, she was able to formulate a treatment plan to aid the couple in testing these assumptions, which were supporting their hopelessness. Conceptualizing the case helped the therapist devise a clearer therapeutic plan. Six weeks later she reported the couple began to make progress once their interfering beliefs were identified and dispelled.

Should a therapist ever give up hope? If a couple decide to end their relationship, the therapist can assist them to evaluate the pros and cons of this decision and then help them carry it out in an adaptive way. If the couple wants to continue to work on their relationship, they have a right to a therapist who will help them do this. If one therapist cannot determine how to accomplish this, it may be necessary to refer the case to another therapist.

The position outlined here on therapist hopefulness may seem extreme. It is stated in this way to guide therapists away from a tendency to give up too easily on challenging cases. Of course situations do exist where it might be reasonable for a therapist to suggest relationship termination as a possible treatment outcome.

This position could be argued in cases where the relationship is clearly destructive for one of the people and the partner is unwilling even to attempt change. If the therapist has tried and failed to engage the destructive partner in the therapy, it might be important to support the participating client in an examination of whether or not the relationship is healthy for the client. A therapist may even need to actively encourage the client to imagine coping outside the relationship if the client is fearful of taking this step.

If both partners have decided they would be happier ending the relationship and come to get help separating, a therapist could assist in this process after a brief examination of the reasons for ending the relationship. If a client does not want to struggle with a long-term relationship in the hope of resolving problems, it may be inappropriate for the therapist to attempt to change this value.

OTHER PSYCHIATRIC
DISORDERS IN THE COUPLE

In addition to the presenting relationship problem, a therapist may identify other psychiatric disorders within the couple - either Axis I (e.g., depression, substance abuse, generalized anxiety disorder) or Axis II (i.e., personality disorders). Sometimes these problems are secondary to the couple's distress and may improve along with the relationship. For example, agoraphobia in one spouse may be serving to keep other issues in the relationship covert. Other times these disorders may be contributing to the couple's difficulties or independently disrupting the relationship.

In most cases, adjunctive individual therapy is recommended to resolve these additional disorders or other problem areas. Ideally, the individual therapy should be conducted by a different therapist from the couple's attending therapist. If this is not practical, the same therapist can do both, although the therapist will need to be careful to specify any limits of confidentiality. There may be complex issues of trust, especially if one or both members of the couple maintain a diagnosis of personality disorder.

The treatment of other disorders with Cognitive Therapy is described elsewhere in books on depression (Beck, Rush, et al., 1979), anxiety disorders (Beck, Emery, et al., 1985; Hawton et al., 1989), and personality disorders (Beck et al., 1990). It is helpful if the therapist working with the couple coordinates treatment with the individual therapist so the conjoint therapy can be adapted to any special needs created by individual problems.

If a member of the couple is depressed, the therapist can expect negativity and hopelessness to color his or her perception of the relationship. Depressed clients often feel overwhelmed and hopeless and generalize this to all aspects of their life. The therapist can help the depressed partner by reducing each of the therapy steps into small pieces to increase the likelihood of compliance and success. Since automatic thought records are a major tool in individual Cognitive Therapy for depression, the depressed member of the couple may actually become quite skilled at identifying and testing negative thoughts about the relationship. In this way, the individual and couples therapy can enhance each other. For a more detailed review of depression and couples therapy, the reader is referred to Beach, Sandeen, and O'Leary (1990).

A client who is anxious can be expected to make catastrophic predictions or worry about different aspects of the relationship. The anxious client may think it is impossible to cope with relationship problems. Again, individual therapy can help test these fears. The couple's therapist can be alert for these types of anxious thoughts and set up small behavioral experiments with skill practice in the sessions to increase the anxious client's confidence in his or her own abilities to cope with problems.

When one or both members of the couple have a personality disorder, the couple's therapist may expect some problem areas to be exacerbated by more rigid beliefs. A woman with an avoidant personality disorder might be reluctant to express anger in the couple's session for fear her husband will be angry and leave her. A man with a borderline personality disorder may continually question whether or not he can trust his girlfriend.

The recent book, *Cognitive Therapy of Personality Disorders* (Beck et al., 1990), outlines methods for each personality disorder which can be adapted for use in couples therapy. If the personality disorder is accompanied by features which are highly disruptive to the couple's work, adjunctive individual therapy may be necessary. Otherwise, some work on the personality disorder can be done concurrently with the couple's work, especially because many personality disorder features are most evident in relationships.

Bob and Jan had been married 3 years when they sought therapy for frequent arguments. These arguments mostly focused on Bob's jealousy when Jan would go out with friends after work. He felt certain she was having an affair although she insisted she was not. Bob reported a variety of symptoms which warranted a diagnosis of borderline personality disorder.

Following the cognitive model for borderline personality disorder (Beck et al., 1990), the therapist conceptualized the problem as resulting from Bob's negative core beliefs: "I'm no good," "People can't be trusted," and "I'm weak and powerless." In addition to these negative schemas, Bob's thinking was severely dichotomous as is typified by borderline personality disorder. Therefore, when Jan went out after work, his mistrust of her combined with his extremely derogatory self-view led him to conclude that this was a danger sign. His dichotomous thinking served to push his fears to the extreme: Each time that Jan would be late, he would conclude that she was having an affair and was going to leave him. Because he felt extremely powerless, this "fact" frightened Bob, and his terror at the prospect of being alone enhanced his rage.

Given this conceptualization, the therapist worked with Bob's jealousy by teaching him to recognize his cognitive distortions, particularly dichotomous thinking. The therapist helped Bob place his negative thoughts on a continuum. Over time, Bob was able to see that Jan showed that she could be trusted in many ways and so she was on the higher quarter of the continuum of trustworthiness. Jan was able to talk with Bob and point out qualities that weakened his view that he was no good. By teaching alternative responses to make when he felt threatened, the therapist helped Bob feel somewhat more in control.

Each of these small shifts with Bob and Jan away from dichotomous thinking and toward continuum thinking helped reduce Bob's jealousy. Although it is beyond the scope of this book to detail the therapy adjustments that need to be made for each personality disorder, this example highlights the utility of a cognitive conceptualization to help adapt the conjoint therapy when the couple has special needs.

CULTURAL ISSUES

Couples enter their relationships with beliefs and expectations that grow from and are supported by their culture. In addition to the broader societal influences, each individual has a personal cultural history which can be conceptualized along four dimensions: ethnic or racial heritage, socioeconomic status, religious or spiritual affiliation, and sex role values (Davis & Padesky, 1989).

Therapists need to be sensitive to assessing these values, especially when the couple are from a different cultural background than the therapist. At a minimum, it enhances therapeutic rapport if the therapist tries to understand the cultural context of the couple's beliefs. At best, understanding the cultural roots of beliefs can help the therapist plan therapeutic changes with knowledge of their personal history and terrain.

One couple entered therapy following a long history of arguments over finances. The therapist explored the socioeconomic history of each and found that Walter had grown up in near poverty and lived with daily anxiety that hard times might come and he would not be able to feed his family. Although this outcome was unlikely given his savings and earning power as an accountant, his fear was a replay of his childhood circumstances when his father had been laid off from work during the Depression. His wife, Maureen, was raised the daughter of a physician and had difficulty imagining the doom that stalked Walter and enraged him when she overspent their budget.

Reviewing their differences in cultural background and the impact that these can have on beliefs and expectations helped this couple feel greater empathy for each other's behavior. They were able to work together more collaboratively on budget planning, taking into account the legitimacy of each person's perspective based on personal economic history.

A Moslem woman came to therapy to get help with her marriage. She came in secret because therapy was not acceptable in her culture. She was depressed and sad about her relationship; the young therapist helping her blamed her depression on her culture and the "oppression of wearing a veil." Fortunately, a supervisor familiar with the client's culture was able to point out to the therapist that wearing a veil is a point of pride to most women in Iran and not a cause for depression. The therapist needed to put aside her own biases in order to hear the client's problem.

GAY AND LESBIAN COUPLES

Gay and lesbian couples seek therapy for the same issues as heterosexual couples, and the same therapy principles apply. Therapists working with gay and lesbian couples should also be familiar with the special pressures and circumstances these couples may face. It is also important that therapists working with lesbian and gay clients familiarize themselves with the myths and realities of these lifestyles (American Psychological Association, 1985).

If gay and lesbian couples are not part of a supportive community of family and friends, they may face the added stress of isolation in times of relationship distress. Heterosexual couples can often turn to friends and co-workers for support and to gather normative data on relationship problems and solutions. If a lesbian couple are in distress they may not be able to mention this strain to co-workers; in fact, only a few friends may even know they are in a relationship.

Until recently (cf. Clunis & Green, 1988) little has been written about normal developmental stages in lesbian or gay relationships. It can be helpful for couples to realize that some of the conflicts they are experiencing are normal. This normative data is even more helpful than for heterosexual couples because gay and lesbian couples do not have role models in the larger culture. In small communities there may be only a few other gay couples with whom to compare experiences.

If one of the partners in a gay couple holds homophobic beliefs or fears, problems in the relationship might be used as an opportunity to say, "I'm probably not gay - that's the problem." A cognitive therapist can help a gay or lesbian client achieve a more positive self-identity (Padesky, 1989). This, in turn, can help the partnership have a greater chance of surviving.

Many male couples face added strain due to the AIDS epidemic. These men may have buried dozens of friends and also lived with the anxiety of potentially facing a fatal illness themselves. One gay man described himself as being "in emotional shock. I have lost so many friends I can hardly cry anymore." Long-time couples may face the guilt common to survivors of disasters. Newer couples may resent having to use safe sex practices even within a committed relationship. And family members who may have been cautiously silent in their nonacceptance of a gay lifestyle may now strongly argue that their gay son or brother should "try to be straight."

These and other issues in gay and lesbian relationships can be addressed well with standard Cognitive Therapy methods as long as the therapist is aware of his or her own beliefs and attitudes about these relationships. Whether the therapist is gay, lesbian, or heterosexual, it is difficult to grow up in a largely heterosexual culture without some biased attitudes toward gay and lesbian relationships. As with all cultures, it is the therapist's responsibility to be educated and supportive of the couple's chosen value system.

7.
CASE VIGNETTE: ZACK AND CARLI*

Zack and Carli were a young couple in their mid-20s who had been married for 3 years with one child, 13 months of age. This was the first marriage for both. Zack was employed as a forklift operator with a local packaging warehouse, and Carli was employed part-time at a bakery where she decorated cakes.

The couple were referred for marriage counseling by their family physician due to constant arguing over what they termed insignificant problems. Both reported the arguing was ongoing for the past year and a half, particularly as a result of Zack's recent cocaine usage (Dattilio, 1990a).

BACKGROUND INFORMATION

Zack and Carli met at a party through mutual friends. They dated only 6 months prior to marrying. Both claimed that their marriage went extremely well until approximately 1-1/2 years into the relationship when Carli discovered Zack was using cocaine on a regular basis. This had occurred after Carli noticed that increasing amounts of money had begun to vanish from the savings account with no explanation. She eventually confronted Zack when he confessed, after much prodding, to his chronic cocaine usage. She demanded that he discontinue his use and seek help.

---

*Note: From "Cognitive Marital Therapy: A Case Study" by F. M. Dattilio, 1990a, *Journal of Family Psychotherapy*, *1*(1), pp. 15-31. Copyright © 1990 by The Haworth Press, Inc. Reprinted by permission.

He made promises to her on several occasions, only to be caught under the influence repeatedly by her. Finally, she threatened to leave him unless he sought professional help immediately. He contacted his family physician who referred him to a rehabilitation program where he remained in residential care for 1 month. Subsequent to his treatment stay, he was released, with weekly follow-up visits that lasted for a duration of 2 months.

At the time of intake for marital therapy, Zack was 3 months post-status. Prior to this episode, both Zack and Carli denied any history of drug or alcohol abuse. They were residing in a townhouse with their daughter, Rebecca.

INITIAL ASSESSMENT

During the initial 2-hour assessment, Zack and Carli were seen together. A complete history of their relationship was obtained, along with details regarding their single lives prior to dating. Information was also gathered regarding their perceptions of their respective parents' marital relationships. Additional information was obtained regarding reasons for seeking treatment, length and duration of the problems, previous attempts at symptom/problem resolution (e.g., previous counseling, self-help programs), social lifestyle, areas of compatibility/incompatibility, relationship with their child, relationship with families of origin, and use of drugs or alcohol.

Aside from the background information, the initial session was devoted to developing a conceptualization of the presenting problem. In this particular case, Zack and Carli agreed that they were bickering and arguing almost constantly, along with dealing with the tension of the potential for Zack relapsing into cocaine usage. Carli described her concern as being a lack of trust in Zack. She constantly questioned his whereabouts and doubted he was completely honest about his use of cocaine and/or other substances (e.g., alcohol). She claimed that as a result of being so shocked by Zack's clandestine use of cocaine, she felt compelled to keep track of his time whenever he left the house. She gave him the "third degree" each time he returned home from being out alone. She also was obsessed with balancing the checkbook and called the bank every week for account balances to insure that he was not withdrawing extra money.

Zack's major complaints were that in his attempts to remain drug-free, Carli's constant investigation and questioning were agitating him. It was during these periods of agitation and arguing that he felt the urge to escape it all by resuming his cocaine usage. Although he understood this would obviously be counterproductive to his recovery and to the marriage, Zack claimed that Carli was driving him back to cocaine use through her nagging and bickering.

During the initial assessment, Zack and Carli were both presented with the *Marital Attitude Questionnaire-Revised* (MAQ-R; Pretzer et al., 1983). Both were instructed to complete the inventory separately and bring it to the next session.

They were also oriented briefly to the cognitive model of marital relationships and marital therapy and were requested to begin reading the first several chapters of *Love Is Never Enough* (Beck, 1988).

Individual appointments were made for Zack and Carli subsequent to the initial assessment.

SECOND SESSION

During this individual session with Carli, her responses to the *Marital Attitudes Questionnaire* were reviewed. The majority of questions she marked with a 1 (strongly agree) fell within the area of a general disbelief that the relationship would change. The items were used as a tool to initiate discussion on the areas of conflict.

Questions were used to ascertain Carli's automatic thoughts about her relationship and the potential for change.

Below are some of the automatic thoughts which she maintained about the relationship:

- "I am so leery of Zack's ability to change."
- "He has lied to me too many times already."
- "I feel as though I was deceived about our entire relationship."
- "I have no idea whether or not he's out there getting high at this very moment."

As can be seen from Carli's automatic thoughts, she maintained a negative frame of her marital relationship. Upon probing her automatic thoughts, her underlying beliefs, or schemas, were uncovered. The primary themes of her schemas were:

- "I have always been unlucky in relationships; I'll never be happy."
- "I set myself up to be used; no one wants to love me."
- "People don't change and it is unrealistic for me to think that Zack will."

The essential goal of this first session with Carli was to develop a clear and detailed conceptualization of how she viewed herself and her marital situation and, most importantly, how she viewed her future in the relationship. It was clear from her statements and beliefs that Carli possessed a negative bias in her thinking which distorted her view, creating a negative frame of the relationship.

As a homework assignment, Carli was asked to begin processing her automatic thoughts through the "Daily Dysfunctional Thoughts" (DDT) sheets to which she was fully oriented during this session (see "Daily Record of Dysfunctional Thoughts," p. 101).

THIRD SESSION

The third session involved an individual assessment with Zack. Here the same format was used as in the individual visit with Carli. Through the use of questioning, Zack's automatic thoughts about the relationship were ascertained.

- "I am trying like hell to stay off of the coke and she's doing everything to drive me back to it."
- "She picks and questions everything."
- "What's the use of trying if I am being accused of it anyway?"
- "I make one mistake and I am pegged as a drug addict for life."

After questioning Zack's automatic thoughts, it was learned that many of his thoughts stemmed from the underlying belief that he could never do anything right as a child. He had made several blunders during his childhood and seemed to receive endless criticism from his father and brothers about it. He even recalled his father making the statement, "Once a klutz, always a klutz."

Zack's underlying beliefs carried the themes:

DAILY RECORD OF DYSFUNCTIONAL THOUGHTS

SITUATION	EMOTION(S)	AUTOMATIC THOUGHT(S)	RATIONAL RESPONSE	OUTCOME
Describe: 1. Actual event leading to unpleasant emotion, or 2. Stream of thoughts, daydream, or recollection, leading to unpleasant emotion.	1. Specify sad/anxious/angry, and so on. 2. Rate degree of emotion, 1-100.	1. Write automatic thought(s) that preceded emotion(s). 2. Rate belief in automatic thought(s), 0-100%.	1. Write rational response to automatic thought(s). 2. Rate belief in rational response, 0-100%.	1. Re-rate belief in automatic thought(s), 0-100%. 2. Specify and rate subsequent emotions, 1-100.
DATE				

EXPLANATION: When you experience an unpleasant emotion, note the situation that seemed to stimulate the emotion. (If the emotion occurred while you were thinking, daydreaming, and so on, please note this.) Then note the automatic thought associated with the emotion. Record the degree to which you believe this thought: 0% = not at all; 100% = completely. In rating degree of emotion: 1 = a trace; 100 = the most intense possible.

- "It's very difficult to be forgiven once you screw up in life."
- "I failed as a son and I am destined to fail as a husband and father."

As a result of this exercise, Zack was helped to understand how his underlying beliefs made him predisposed to automatic thoughts that he would fail at his attempts to change. It infiltrated his interaction with Carli, contributing to much of the tension in their relationship.

Note: It appeared that an essential key to reaching the core dynamics in this relationship was to defuse the immediate tension which existed concerning trust and honesty. It was felt that unless this was accomplished, further headway could prove difficult since all the tension would tend to revert to this area of conflict.

FOURTH SESSION

The fourth session included both Zack and Carli. The agenda involved reviewing the cognitive model and placing specific emphasis on the "cognitive distortions" that occur in marital interactions. These were explained as types of fallacious thinking that contributed to the feedback loops supporting marital dysfunction in communication. (Please refer back to "Cognitive Distortions" in Chapter 2.) Below is a list of errors that existed in Zack and Carli's reasoning:

1. *Arbitrary Inferences*. Zack arrived home a half-hour late from work and Carli concluded, "He was probably out making a deal somewhere."
2. *Selective Abstraction*. Carli failed to answer Zack's greeting the first thing in the morning and he concluded, "She must be angry at me again."
3. *Overgeneralization*. After having an argument with Zack, Carli stated, "All men are alike."
4. *Magnification and Minimization*. Zack viewed the trouble with his marriage and stated, "My entire life is a shamble."
5. *Personalization*. Zack stated to himself, "All my friends have always been losers - I guess I am really a loser too!"
6. *Dichotomous Thinking*. "Because Zack has done drugs, that makes him untrustworthy in every dimension."

7. *Labeling and Mislabeling.* Subsequent to continual mistakes in meal preparation, Carli stated, "I am worthless" as opposed to recognizing her error as being human.

These errors were highlighted in the session in attempts to have Zack and Carli become aware of the distortions in their thinking. In addition, the cognitive model was explained to them in specific detail.

Subsequent to this review of the overall model and the common types of cognitive distortions, it was also explained to them that, as a result of the gradual deterioration in the relationship, they had both come to view each other in a negative frame. That is, those qualities they once had admired in each other were now viewed as being undesirable and created a negative light they shone on each other. The outline below delineates the flip side of Zack and Carli's frames extracted from them during the individual interviews:

Zack's View of Carli

Carli's Positive Qualities	Carli's Negative Qualities
-- Supportive	-- Nagging
-- Thrifty	-- Tightwad
-- Energetic	-- Hyper
-- Principled	-- Unforgiving

Carli's View of Zack

Zack's Positive Qualities	Zack's Negative Qualities
-- Fun-loving	-- Parties too much
-- Loyal	-- Too devoted to
-- Free-spirited	his buddies
-- Has a way with words	-- Can't be trusted
	-- Is a liar

The therapist then proceeded with the session addressing the conflict at hand with both partners:

Therapist: Okay, now I'd like to focus on the conflict which seems to be the foremost issue - your trust, Carli, in Zack's ability to remain free of substance use, and

103

Zack's fear of giving in as a result of retaliating against Carli.

Carli: That's right. Right now I am extremely skeptical because he has lied to me so much. I really doubt that he'll change, and I emotionally cannot afford to be burned any longer.

Therapist: So you, Carli, are not very optimistic about this entire counseling process. What about you, Zack?

Zack: Well, I think that she's being unfair. I don't know what the hell she wants. I went through rehabilitation! I've stayed clean for almost 3 months now. She just won't stay off my back.

Carli: (Interrupting) That's right. Not when you say you're coming home at 5:30 and you come strolling in at a quarter to seven. What am I supposed to think?

Therapist: Okay. Look we need to hear each other out. It won't be a very productive session if you fall into the pattern of arguing again. So could we establish a ground rule that we will not interrupt each other when speaking?

Zack: Yeah, I'll agree to it. But she's the one who can't stop her mouth.

Therapist: Well, I'll get to her in a minute Zack, but I want an agreement from you.

Zack: Sure, you have my word.

Therapist: Okay. Now, Carli, do you think that you can agree to this?

Carli: I don't know. He just lies so damn much. I just have a lot of trouble sitting here listening to some of these statements.

Therapist: Well, then let's do this. Would you, Carli, be willing to write down your thoughts, or what we call your automatic thoughts, when you hear these statements that Zack makes?

Carli: You mean right now?

Therapist: Yes, right now in the session. The same way I had you do when we met individually.

Carli: I guess so.

Therapist: Now, I'd like you to take your pen and notepad and write down the automatic thoughts that you had when Zack made his last statement. I think the statement was, "I went through rehabilitation and have stayed clean for more than 3 months. She just won't stay off my back."

(Carli takes a few minutes to write down her automatic thoughts.)

Carli: All right, here they are.
Therapist: Carli, will you read them out loud.
Carli:
1. Yes, big deal, 3 months and he thinks he's kicked the habit.
2. As soon as I start to let my guard down, he'll be right back doing the stuff again.
3. "What do I want" he says. I just want him to stay clean so that he doesn't ruin our entire marriage.
4. Every time that he goes out with those damn friends of his, he takes a step closer to relapse.

Therapist: Okay, good. Now, Carli, I'd like you to weigh the evidence for each one of those statements that you made and balance them with an alternative thought right next to it. I would also like you to label the distortion according to the terms that we discussed earlier. For example, let's take your first thought: "Big deal, 3 months and he thinks that he's kicked the habit." Now what evidence do you have that supports the notion that he believes that he has it made, that he's remained clean for 3 months?

Carli: Well, none really. Just his cocky attitude.
Therapist: Is it cocky? Or is he maintaining a confident attitude?
Carli: Well, confident actually.
Therapist: All right, so just because he's acting confident doesn't mean that he feels that he has it made, does it?
Carli: No, I really have no evidence to back that up.
Therapist: And how would you label this distorted thought according to our model?
Carli: Probably a combination of "Selective Abstraction" and "Mislabeling."
Therapist: That's right! So how might you write your alternative thought?
Carli: Well, let's see:
1. Actually, 3 months is pretty good so far. This has been his longest dry period. I guess the positive attitude is a key force in his staying clean. Maybe it's a good sign.

Therapist: Okay, not bad! Now, I'd like you to do the same thing with the rest of your thoughts.

(The therapist has Carli write an alternative response to her thoughts after weighing the evidence in front of Zack, so that he can witness her efforts in balancing out her self-statements. The remainder of her thoughts are below with the cognitive distortion identified)*

Automatic Thought	Cognitive Distortion	Alternative Thought
"As soon as I start to let my guard down, he'll be right back to doing coke again."	Overgeneralization	"I really have no evidence to support this. Perhaps letting my guard down a bit might help to give him some reinforcement for staying clean."
"I want him to stay clean so that he doesn't ruin our marriage."	Magnification	"I need to give him a chance. He's remained clean for 3 months, which is something. If he has a relapse, it doesn't mean that he ruins our entire marriage."
"Every time he goes out with those damn friends of his, he takes a step closer to relapse."	Selective Abstraction	"This isn't necessarily so. The control has to be within him. It's not where he goes, but what he tells himself. The more that I am supportive to him, the less he may be inclined to go out and use cocaine."

---

*For the sake of brevity, this excerpt was edited. The actual restructuring process took much longer due to Carli's resistance and rigidity.

Therapist: Now, Zack, let's take a look at the automatic thoughts that you had during that same conversation we had just a few minutes ago. What were your thoughts?

Zack: Well, I thought:
1. God, there she goes. She just can't get it through her head to lay off.
2. Sometimes I believe that she almost wants me to fail.
3. If I fail, then I blow it. The marriage is over.

Therapist: All right, now can you balance your negative automatic thoughts with alternatives in the same manner that Carli has done?

Automatic Thought	Cognitive Distortion	Alternative Thought
"There she goes. She just can't get it through her head to lay off."	Arbitrary Inference	"This is Carli's way of expressing herself. It doesn't mean that she is necessarily condemning me."
"Sometimes I believe that she almost wants me to fail."	Personalization	"That's ridiculous. If she wanted to end the marriage, then she'd do that, not set me up for failure."
"If I fail, I blow it, the marriage is over."	Dichotomous Thinking	"If I fail, then I get back on my horse and try again. It doesn't necessarily mean that the world comes to an end."

(By allowing both partners to witness the restructuring of automatic thoughts, they view each other in a positive light - as they hear themselves rehearse the positive "flip side" of their thoughts. They are also able to witness each other make a concerted effort to view things in a different light; this often has a positive impact on their respective view of the other.)

Therapist: All right now, as a result of this little exercise, what are you both thinking right now?

Zack: Well, personally, I feel as though she is able to see the optimistic side of my situation, but I am still a little leery about whether or not she'll stick with that. It will probably change back to the negative as soon as we leave here.

Carli: I feel the same way. It was good to hear him say something different for a change, but I still don't trust him.

Therapist: Surely the more permanent changes will come in time; however, the point in this session is to help you both to see that by monitoring your thoughts and making some adjustments, you can both envision how things can change. As a homework assignment, I would like you to continue with this exercise, particularly each time you begin to become angry with each other. In addition, I would like you to both take these blank stickers and each wear about 5 or 10 of them on your clothes while lounging around the house. Each time one of you feels that your spouse has made a comment which was either positive or complimentary toward you, I would like you to remove a sticker from his or her clothing.

Carli: This is sort of childish, don't you think?

Therapist: Well, perhaps, but I think you might be surprised with how you feel when you try it.

(The therapist schedules the appointments no more than 1 week apart so that enough time is allocated for the assignment to be completed, yet not too much time elapses.)

SIXTH SESSION

The sixth session was a follow-up to the previous session's assignment. Both Zack and Carli had claimed that for the most part their week had gone relatively smoothly except for a minor blow-up which had occurred just prior to coming to the therapy session. When their argument was re-analyzed in the therapy session, it was determined that their conflict had come as a result of deviating from their structured assignment and reverting to their negative frames. The couple were encouraged to review this heated event and analyze their automatic thoughts again, applying the techniques of writing an alternative view, weighing the evidence, and identifying their cognitive distortions.

One of the additional techniques that was introduced was "testing the predictions." During the week between sessions, Carli had noticed that $50 had been withdrawn from the savings account by Zack with no explanation to her. Carli stated that she was certain that Zack had used it to buy drugs but anticipated another fight upon confronting him about it. The therapist had her "test the prediction" by practicing nonthreatening ways of confronting Zack and then actually questioning him about the money. When she did so, Zack explained to her that he needed a new pair of work boots and withdrew money one morning to buy them. He supported his explanation by showing her the receipt.

Once their situation was defused to the point where they could get along in a reasonable manner, they were then administered additional inventories which included: *Problems in the Partnership* (Beck, 1988) and *Problems in the Style of Communication* (Beck, 1988). This allowed Zack and Carli to pinpoint additional areas of conflict and develop a future course for direction in therapy.

SUBSEQUENT SESSIONS

As the conflicts began to subside, Zack was able to concentrate on improving his performance and avoiding the temptation of cocaine use. He was referred back for outpatient follow-up counseling sessions with the rehabilitation clinic. Both Zack and Carli were also encouraged to attend a couples' support group for substance abusers through the same clinic.

Subsequently, the sessions focused on the dependency needs of each and their actual fears of failing in their relationship. The duration of treatment was 6 months, with a total of 20 sessions. A 1-year follow-up showed both partners enjoying a relatively peaceful relationship with no relapse of substance abuse.

SUMMARY

This case focuses on a marital situation which may have led to divorce had the couple not entered treatment.

The cognitive approach was successful in defusing the conflict situation, allowing the couple to begin to deal with the deeper issues in their relationship.

8.
CONCLUDING REMARKS

The old adage, "It's easier said than done," applies directly to the field of counseling and psychotherapy. It is also much easier to read about various techniques and interventions than it is to actually implement them.

It is our hope that this book has given the reader a basic working knowledge of Cognitive Therapy with Couples. It is important to note that, like anything else, newly acquired skills require practice. Therefore, the tools that are described in this book will best serve the practitioner who allows an appropriate amount of time and patience for them to become a familiar part of his or her skill repertoire.

The specific techniques may also be used separately from the overall model, thus allowing the practitioner to add to another therapy model rather than being compelled to adopt the model as a whole. At the very least, these techniques serve as excellent defusing agents, particularly with volatile couples. If used to their fullest extent (involving philosophy and theory), they can be an even more powerful tool and provide the practitioner with an excellent framework for case conceptualization and intervention techniques.

REFERENCES

Abrahms, J. L. (1982, November). *Inducing a Collaborative Set in Distressed Couples: Nonspecific Therapist-Patient Issues in Cognitive Therapy.* Paper presented at the Annual Meeting of the Association for the Advancement of Behavior Therapy, Los Angeles, CA.

Abrahms, J. (1983). Cognitive-behavioral strategies to enhance a collaborative set in distressed couples. In A. Freeman (Ed.), *Cognitive Therapy with Couples and Groups* (pp. 125-156). New York: Plenum.

Abrahms, J., & Spring, M. (1989). The flip-flop factor. *International Cognitive Therapy Newsletter, 5*(1), 1, 7-8.

Adler, A. (1936). The neurotic's picture of the world. *International Journal of Individual Psychology, 2*, 3-10.

American Psychological Association. (1985). *A Selected Bibliography of Lesbian and Gay Concerns in Psychology: An Affirmative Perspective.* Washington, DC: Author.

Arnold, M. (1960). *Emotions and Personality* (Vol. 1). New York: Columbia University Press.

Aylmer, R. (1986). Bowen family systems marital therapy. In N. S. Jacobson & A. S. Gurman (Eds.), *Clinical Handbook of Marital Therapy.* New York: Guilford.

Azrin, N. H., Naster, B. J., & Jones, R. (1973). A rapid learning-based procedure for marital counseling. *Behavior Research and Therapy, 11*, 365-382.

Bandura, A. (1977). *Social Learning Theory.* Englewood Cliffs, NJ: Prentice-Hall.

113

Baucom, D. H. (1981, November). *Cognitive Behavioral Strategies in the Treatment of Marital Discord.* Paper presented at the Annual Meeting of the Association for the Advancement of Behavior Therapy, Toronto, Canada.

Baucom, D., & Epstein, N. (1990). *Cognitive-Behavioral Marital Therapy.* New York: Brunner/Mazel.

Beach, S. R. H., Sandeen, E. E., & O'Leary, K. D. (1990). *Depression in Marriage: A Model for Etiology and Treatment.* New York: Guilford.

Beck, A. T. (1963). Thinking and depression: 1. Idiosyncratic content and cognitive distortions. *Archives of General Psychiatry, 9,* 324-333.

Beck, A. T. (1964). Thinking and depression: 2. Theory and therapy. *Archives of General Psychiatry, 10,* 561-571.

Beck, A. T. (1967). *Depression: Clinical, Experimental, and Theoretical Aspects.* New York: Hoeber. (Republished as *Depression: Causes and Treatment.* Philadelphia: University of Pennsylvania Press, 1972)

Beck, A. T. (1970). Cognitive therapy: Nature and relation to behavior therapy. *Behavior Therapy, 1,* 184-200.

Beck, A. T. (1976). *Cognitive Therapy and the Emotional Disorders.* New York: International Universities Press.

Beck, A. T. (1986, June 28). Treating depression: Can we talk? [Letter to the Editor]. *Science News,* p. 12.

Beck, A. T. (1988). *Love Is Never Enough.* New York: Harper & Row.

Beck, A. T., & Emery, G. (1979). *Cognitive Therapy of Anxiety and Phobic Disorders.* Philadelphia: Center for Cognitive Therapy.

Beck, A. T., Emery, G., & Greenberg, R. (1985). *Anxiety and Phobias: A Cognitive Approach.* New York: Basic Books.

Beck, A. T., Epstein, N., Brown, G., & Steer, R. A. (1985, November). *An Inventory of Measuring Clinical Anxieties.* Paper presented at the Annual Meeting of the Association for Advancement of Behavior Therapy, Houston, TX.

Beck, A. T., Freeman, A., Pretzer, J., Fleming, B., Davis, D., Ottaviani, R., Beck, J., Simon, K., Padesky, C., Meyer, J., & Trexler, L. (1990). *Cognitive Therapy of Personality Disorders.* New York: Guilford.

Beck, A. T., Kovacs, M., & Weisman, A. (1979). Assessment of suicidal intention: The scale for suicidal ideation. *Journal of Consulting and Clinical Psychology, 47,* 343-352.

Beck, A. T., Laude, R., & Bohnert, M. (1974). Ideation components of anxiety neurosis. *Archives of General Psychiatry, 31,* 319-325.

Beck, A. T., & Padesky, C. (1987, May). *New Directions in Cognitive Therapy.* Workshop presented in Seattle, WA.

Beck, A. T., & Rush, A. J. (1978). Cognitive approaches to depression and suicide. In G. Servan (Ed.), *Cognitive Defects in the Development of Mental Illness* (pp. 235-257). New York: Brunner/Mazel. (Published under the auspices of Kitty Foundation)

Beck, A. T., Rush, A. J., Shaw, B. F., & Emery, G. (1979). *Cognitive Therapy of Depression.* New York: Guilford.

Beck, A. T., Schuyler, D., & Herman, I. (1974). Development of suicidal intent scales. In A. T. Beck, H. L. P. Resnik, & D. J. Lettieri (Eds.), *The Prediction of Suicide* (pp. 45-46). Bowie, MD: Charles Press.

Beck, A. T., Ward, C. H., Mendelson, M., Mock, J. E., & Erbaugh, J. K. (1961). An inventory for measuring depression. *Archives of General Psychiatry, 4,* 561-571.

Beck, A. T., Weisman, A., Lester, D., & Trexler, L. (1974). The measurement of pessimism: The hopelessness scale. *Journal of Consulting and Clinical Psychology, 42,* 861-865.

Blackburn, I. M., Bishop, S., Glen, A. M., Wholley, L. J., & Christie, J. E. (1981). The efficacy of cognitive therapy in depression: A treatment trial using cognitive therapy and psychotherapy, each alone and in combination. *British Journal of Psychiatry, 139,* 181-189.

Burns, D. (1980). *Feeling Good: The New Mood Therapy.* New York: Signet.

Burns, D. (1989). *Feeling Good Handbook.* New York: William Morrow & Co.

Butcher, J., Dahlstrom, W. G., Graham, J. R., & Tellegen, A. (1989). *The Minnesota Multiphasic Personality Inventory-2.* Minneapolis: University of Minnesota Press.

Clunis, D. M., & Green, G. D. (1988). *Lesbian Couples.* Seattle, WA: The Seal Press.

Dattilio, F. M. (1987). The use of paradoxical intention in the treatment of panic attacks. *Journal of Counseling and Development, 66,* 102-103.

Dattilio, F. M. (1988). Relation of experience in sex and panic: A preliminary note. *The Cognitive-Behaviorist, 10,* 3-4.

Dattilio, F. M. (1989a). A guide to cognitive martial therapy. In P. A. Keller & S. R. Heyman (Eds.), *Innovations in Clinical*

Practice: *A Source Book* (Vol. 8, pp. 27-42). Sarasota, FL: Professional Resource Exchange.

Dattilio, F. M. (1989b). Cognitive therapy with distressed couples: Part One. *Clinical Advances in the Treatment of Psychiatric Disorders, 3*(4), 1-10.

Dattilio, F. M. (1989c). Cognitive therapy with distressed couples: Part Two. *Clinical Advances in the Treatment of Psychiatric Disorders, 3,* 10 and 16.

Dattilio, F. M. (1990a). Cognitive marital therapy: A case study. *Journal of Family Psychotherapy, 1,* 15-31.

Dattilio, F. M. (1990b). Symptom induction and decatastrophization in the treatment of panic. *Journal of Mental Health Counseling, 12,* 515-519.

Davis, D., & Padesky, C. (1989). Enhancing cognitive therapy with women. In A. Freeman, K. Simon, L. Beutler, & H. Arkowitz (Eds.), *Comprehensive Handbook of Cognitive Therapy* (pp. 535-557). New York: Plenum.

Doherty, W. J. (1981). Cognitive processes in intimate conflict: 1. Extending attribution theory. *American Journal of Family Therapy, 9,* 5-13.

Edwards, D. (1989). Cognitive restructuring through guided imagery: Lessons from Gestalt therapy. In A. Freeman, K. Simon, L. Beutler, & H. Arkowitz (Eds.), *Comprehensive Handbook of Cognitive Therapy* (pp. 283-297). New York: Plenum.

Ellis, A. (1954). *The American Sexual Tragedy.* New York: Twayne and Grove Press. (Revised edition, New York: Lyle Stuart and Grove Press, 1962)

Ellis, A. (1962). *Reason and Emotion in Psychotherapy.* New York: Lyle Stuart.

Ellis, A. (1973). Are cognitive-behavior and rational-emotive therapy synonymous? *Rational Living, 8,* 8-11.

Ellis, A. (1977). The nature of disturbed marital interactions. In A. Ellis & R. Grieger (Eds.), *Handbook of Rational-Emotive Therapy.* New York: Springer.

Ellis, A. (1980). Rational-emotive therapy and cognitive-behavior therapy: Similarities and differences. *Cognitive Therapy and Research, 4,* 325-340.

Ellis, A., & Harper, R. A. (1961). *A Guide to a Successful Marriage.* North Hollywood, CA: Wilshire Books.

Ellis, A., Sichel, J. L., Yeager, R. J., DiMattia, D. J., & Digiuseppe, R. (1989). *Rational-Emotive Couples Therapy, Psychology Practitioners Guidebooks.* New York: Pergamon.

Epstein, N. (1982). Cognitive therapy with couples. *The American Journal of Family Therapy, 10,* 5-16.

Epstein, N. (1986). Cognitive marital therapy: A multilevel assessment and intervention. *Journal of Rational-Emotive Therapy, 4,* 68-81.

Epstein, N., & Eidelson, R. J. (1981). Unrealistic beliefs of clinical couples: Their relationship to expectations, goals and satisfaction. *American Journal of Family Therapy 9,* 13-22.

Fincham, F., & O'Leary, D. K. (1983). Casual inferences for spouse behavior in maritally distressed and nondistressed couples. *Journal of Social and Clinical Psychology, 1,* 42-57.

Finkelhor, D., Gelles, R., Hotaling, G., & Straus, M. (Eds.). (1983). *The Dark Side of Families.* Beverly Hills, CA: Sage.

Freeman, A., & White, D. (1989). Cognitive therapy of suicide. In A. Freeman, K. M. Simon, H. Arkowitz, & L. Beutler (Eds.), *Comprehensive Handbook of Cognitive Therapy.* New York: Plenum.

Gangley, A. (1981). *Participant and Trainer's Manual for Working with Men Who Batter.* Washington, DC: Center for Women Policy Studies.

Geiss, S. K., & O'Leary, K. D. (1981). Therapists ratings of frequency and severity of marital problems: Implications for research. *Journal of Marital & Family Therapy, 7,* 515-520.

Gelles, R. J. (1972). *The Violent Home: A Study of Physical Aggression Between Husbands and Wives.* Beverly Hills, CA: Sage.

Gottman, J., Notarius, C., Gonso, J., & Markman, H. (1976). *A Couples Guide to Communication.* Champaign, IL: Research Press.

Hawton, K., Salkovskis, P., Kirk, J., & Clark, D. (Eds.). (1989). *Cognitive-Behavior Therapy for Psychiatric Problems: A Practical Guide.* Oxford: Oxford University Press.

Hollon, S. D., DeRubeis, R. J., Evans, M. D., Tauson, V. B., Wiemer, M. J., & Garvey, M. J. (1985). *Combined Cognitive-Pharmacotherapy Versus Cognitive Therapy Alone in the Treatment of Depressed Outpatients: Differential Treatment Outcomes in the CPT Projects.* Unpublished manuscript, University of Minnesota and St. Paul-Ramsey Medical Center, Minneapolis-St. Paul, MN.

Holtzworth-Munroe, A., & Jacobson, N. S. (1985). Casual attributions of married couples: When do they search for causes? What do they conclude when they do? *Journal of Personality and Social Psychology, 48,* 1398-1412.

117

Horney, K. (1950). *Neurosis and Human Growth: The Struggle Towards Self-Realization*. New York: Norton.

Jacobson, N. S. (1983). Beyond empiricism: The politics of marital therapy. *American Journal of Family Therapy, 11,* 11-24.

Jacobson, N. S. (1984). A component analysis of behavioral marital therapy: The relative effectiveness of behavior exchange and problem solving training. *Journal of Consulting and Clinical Psychology, 52,* 295-305.

Jacobson, N. S., & Margolin, G. (1979). *Marital Therapy: Strategies Based on Social Learning and Behavior Exchange Principles*. New York: Brunner/Mazel.

Jacobson, N. S., McDonald, D. W., Follette, W. C., & Berley, R. A. (1985). Attributional processes in distressed and nondistressed married couples. *Cognitive Therapy and Research, 9,* 35-50.

Kelly, G. A. (1955). *The Psychology of Personal Constructs*. New York: Norton.

Kelly, J. (1988). Long-term adjustment in children of divorce: Converging findings and implications for practice. *Journal of Family Psychology, 2,* 119-140.

Kovacs, M., & Beck, A. T. (1979). Cognitive-affective processes in depression. In C. E. Izard (Ed.), *Emotions in Personality and Psychopathology* (pp. 417-442). New York: Plenum.

Kovacs, M., Rush, A. J., Beck, A. T., & Hollon, S. D. (1981). Depressed outpatients treated with cognitive therapy or pharmacotherapy: A one-year follow-up. *Archives of General Psychiatry, 38,* 33-39.

Lazarus, R. (1966). *Psychological stress and the coping process*. New York: McGraw-Hill.

Lazarus, A. (1985). *Marital Myths*. San Luis Obispo, CA: Impact Publishers.

Liberman, R. P. (1970). Behavioral approaches to family and couple therapy. *American Journal of Orthopsychiatry, 40,* 106-118.

Liberman, R. P., Wheeler, E., & Sanders, N. (1976). Behavioral therapy for marital disharmony: An educational approach. *Journal of Marriage and Family Counseling, 2,* 383-395.

Mahoney, M. J. (1974). *Cognition and Behavior Modification*. Cambridge, MA: Ballinger.

Mahoney, M., & Lyddon, W. (1988). Recent development in cognitive approaches to counseling and psychotherapy. *Counseling Psychology, 16,* 190-234.

Margolin, G. (1983). Behavior marital therapy: Is there a place for passion, play, and other non-negotiable dimensions? *Behavior Therapist, 6,* 65-68.

Margolin, G., Christensen, A., & Weiss, R. L. (1975). Contracts, cognition, and change: A behavioral approach to marriage therapy. *Counseling Psychologist, 5,* 15-25.

Margolin, G., & Weiss, R. L. (1978). Comparitive evaluation of therapeutic components associated with behavioral marital treatments. *Journal of Consulting and Clinical Psychology, 46,* 1476-1486.

Marlatt, A., & Gordon, J. (Eds.). (1985). *Relapse Prevention: Maintenance Strategies in Addictive Behavior Change.* New York: Guilford.

McKay, M., Rogers, P., & McKay, J. (1989). *When Anger Hurts: Quieting the Storm Within.* Oakland, CA: New Harbinger Publications.

Meichenbaum, D. (1977). *Cognitive-Behavior Modification: An Integrative Approach.* New York: Plenum.

Murphy, G. E., Simmons, A. D., Wetzel, R. D., & Lustman, P. J. (1984). Cognitive therapy versus tricyclic antidepressants in major depression. *Archives of General Psychiatry, 41,* 33-41.

Neidig, P., & Friedman, D. (1984). *Spouse Abuse: A Treatment Program for Couples.* Champaign, IL: Research Press.

NiCarthy, G. (1982). *Getting Free: A Handbook for Women in Abusive Relationships.* Seattle, WA: The Seal Press.

NiCarthy, J., Merriam, K., & Coffman, S. (1984). *Talking It Out: A Guide for Groups for Abused Women.* Seattle, WA: The Seal Press.

Ottaviani, R., & Beck, A. T. (1987). Cognitive aspects of panic disorder. *Journal of Anxiety Disorders, 1,* 15-28.

Padesky, C. (1986, November). *Fundamentals of Cognitive Therapy of Depression.* Workshop presented in Costa Mesa, California.

Padesky, C. (1989). Attaining and maintaining positive lesbian self-identity: A cognitive therapy approach. *Women & Therapy, 8,* 145-156.

Pagelow, M. (1981). *Women Battering: Victims and Their Experiences.* Beverly Hills, CA: Sage.

Patterson, C. H. (1980). *Theories of Counseling and Psychotherapy* (3rd ed.). New York: Harper & Row.

Patterson, C. H. (1986). *Theories of Counseling and Psychotherapy* (4th ed.). New York: Harper & Row.

Patterson, G. R., & Hops, H. (1972). Coercion, a game for two: Intervention techniques for marital conflict. In R. E. Ulrich & P. Montjoy (Eds.), *The Experimental Analysis of Social Behavior* (pp. 424-440). New York: Appleton-Century-Crofts.

Persons, J. (1989). *Cognitive Therapy in Practice: A Case Formulation Approach.* New York: Norton.

Persons, J., Burns, D., & Perloff, J. (1988). Predictors of dropout and outcome in cognitive therapy for depression in a private practice setting. *Cognitive Therapy and Research, 12,* 557-575.

Pretzer, J., & Fleming, B. (1989). Cognitive-behavioral treatment of personality disorders. *The Behavior Therapist, 12*(5), 105-109.

Pretzer, J., Fleming, B., & Epstein, N. (1983, August). *Cognitive Factors in Marital Interaction: The Role of Specific Attributions.* Paper presented at the World Congress of Behavior Therapy, Washington, DC.

Primakoff, L., Epstein, N., & Covi, L. (1986). Homework compliance: An uncontrolled variable in cognitive therapy outcome research. *Behavior Therapy, 17,* 443-446.

Raven, B., Centers, R., & Rodrigues, A. (1975). The bases of conjugal power. In R. E. Cromwell & D. H. Olson (Eds.), *Power in Families.* New York: John Wiley and Sons.

Revenstorf, D. (1984). The role of attribution of marital distress in therapy. In K. Hahlweg & N. S. Jacobson (Eds.), *Marital Interaction: Analysis and Modification* (pp. 309-324). New York: Guilford.

Ritter, K. Y. (1985). The cognitive therapies. *Journal of Counseling and Development, 64,* 42-46.

Rush, A. J., Beck, A. T., Kovacs, M., & Hollon, S. D. (1977). Comparative efficacy of cognitive therapy and pharmacotherapy in the treatment of depressed outpatients. *Cognitive Therapy and Research, 1,* 17-37.

Saunders, D. (1982). Counseling the violent husband. In P. A. Keller & L. G. Ritt (Eds.), *Innovations in Clinical Practice: A Source Book* (Vol. 1, pp. 16-29). Sarasota, FL: Professional Resource Exchange.

Schindler, L., & Vollmer, M. (1984). Cognitive perspectives in behavioral marital therapy: Some proposals for bridging theory, research, and practice. In K. Hahlweg & N. S. Jacobson (Eds.), *Marital Interaction: Analysis and Modification* (pp. 309-324). New York: Guilford.

Schlesinger, S. E., & Epstein, N. (1986). Cognitive-behavioral techniques in marital therapy. In P. A. Keller & L. G. Ritt (Eds.), *Innovations in Clinical Practice: A Source Book* (Vol. 5, pp. 137-154). Sarasota, FL: Professional Resource Exchange.

Schmaling, K. B., Fruzzetti, A. E., & Jacobson, N. S. (1989). Marital problems. In K. Hawton, P. M. Salkovskis, J. Kirk, & D. M. Clark (Eds.), *Cognitive Behavior Therapy for Psychiatric Problems: A Practical Guide* (pp. 339-369). Oxford: Oxford University Press.

Smith, D. (1982). Trends in counseling and psychotherapy. *American Psychologist, 37*, 802-809.

Snyder, D. K. (1981). *Marital Satisfaction Inventory (MSI) Manual*. Los Angeles: Western Psychological Services.

Sonkin, D., & Durphy, M. (1982). *Learning to Live Without Violence: A Handbook for Men*. San Francisco: Volcano Press.

Spainer, G. B. (1976). Measuring dyadic adjustment: New scales for assessing the quality of marriage and similar dyads. *Journal of Marriage and the Family, 38*, 15-28.

Spitzer, R. L., Williams, J. B. W., & Gibbon, M. (1987). *Instruction Manual for the Structured Clinical Interview for DSM-III-R (SCID)*. Biometrics Research Department, New York State Psychiatric Institute, 722 West 168th Street, New York, NY 10032.

Stuart, R. B. (1969). Operant-interpersonal treatment for marital discord. *Journal of Consulting and Clinical Psychology, 33*, 675-682.

Stuart, R. B. (1976). Operant-interpersonal treatment for marital discord. In D. H. L. Olson (Ed.), *Treating Relationships*. Lake Mills, IA: Graphic Press.

Stuart, R. (1980). *Helping Couples Change: A Social Learning Approach to Marital Therapy*. New York: Guilford.

Tyler, T., & Devinitz, V. (1981). Self-serving bias in the attribution of responsibility: Cognitive vs. motivational explanations. *Journal of Experimental Social Psychology, 17*, 408-416.

Walker, L. E. (1979). *The Battered Woman*. New York: Harper & Row.

Walker, L. E. (1984). *The Battered Woman Syndrome*. New York: Springer.

Weiss, R. L. (1980). Strategic behavioral marital therapy: Toward a model for assessment and intervention. In J. P.

Vincent (Ed.), *Advances in Family Intervention, Assessment, and Theory* (Vol. 1, pp. 229-271). Greenwich, CT: JAI Press.

Weiss, R. L. (1984). Cognitive and strategic interventions in behavioral marital therapy. In K. Hahlweg & N. S. Jacobson (Eds.), *Marital Interaction: Analysis and Modification* (pp. 337-355). New York: Guilford.

Weiss, R. L., & Correto, M. C. (1980). The Marital Status Inventory: Development of a measure of dissolution potential. *American Journal of Family Therapy, 8,* 80-95.

Wood, L. F., & Jacobson, N. S. (in press). Clinical applications of behavioral marital therapy. In D. H. Barlow (Ed.), *Behavioral Treatment of Adult Disorders.* New York: Guilford.

Yost-Ritter, K. (1985). The cognitive therapies: An overview for counselors. *Journal of Counseling and Development, 64,* 42-46.

INDEX

A

F

G

H

I

O

P

S

V

W

Y

TO THE OWNER OF THIS BOOK

We hope that you have enjoyed *Cognitive Therapy With Couples*. We would like to know as much about your experiences with this book as possible. Only through your comments and those of others can we learn how to improve it for future readers.

Name_____ Profession_____

1. What I liked most about this book is_____
   _____
   _____

2. What I liked least about this book is_____
   _____
   _____

3. My specific suggestions for improving the book are_____
   _____
   _____

4. Would you recommend this book to your colleagues?_____
   _____
   If not, why?_____
   _____

5. Additional Comments_____
   _____
   _____
   _____
   _____

Please Mail To:

Frank M. Dattilio, PhD
Center for Cognitive Therapy
University of Pennsylvania
133 South 36th Street
Philadelphia, PA 19104

Christine A. Padesky, PhD
Center for Cognitive Therapy
1101 Dove Street
Suite 240
Newport Beach, CA 92660

If you found this book useful . . .

You might want to know more about our other titles.

For a complete listing of all of our publications, please write, call, or fax the following information to the address and phone number listed below:

Name:_____
(Please print)

Address:_____

Address:_____

City/State/Zip:_____

Telephone:(_____)_____

Profession (check all that apply):

_____ Psychologist   _____ Mental Health Counselor
_____ Psychiatrist   _____ Marriage and Family Therapist
_____ School Psychologist   _____ Not in Mental Health Field
_____ Clinical Social Worker _____ Other:_____

◆   ◆   ◆

Professional Resource Press
P.O. Box 15560
Sarasota, FL 34277-1560

Telephone #941-366-7913
FAX #941-366-7971

CTC/1/96

If you or a colleague would like to receive more information on our publications, please mail the completed form to the address below, and we will be happy to send you our latest catalog.

Add Your Name To Our Mailing List

Name:_____
(Please print)

Address:_____

Address:_____

City/State/Zip:_____

Telephone:(_____)_____

I am a:

_____ Psychologist   _____ Mental Health Counselor
_____ Psychiatrist   _____ Marriage and Family Therapist
_____ School Psychologist   _____ Not in Mental Health Field
_____ Clinical Social Worker   _____ Other:_____

Add A Colleague To Our Mailing List

Name:_____
(Please print)

Address:_____

Address:_____

City/State/Zip:_____

Telephone:(_____)_____

I am a:

_____ Psychologist   _____ Mental Health Counselor
_____ Psychiatrist   _____ Marriage and Family Therapist
_____ School Psychologist   _____ Not in Mental Health Field
_____ Clinical Social Worker   _____ Other:_____

Mail To: Professional Resource Press
P.O. Box 15560
Sarasota, FL 34277-1560

If you or a colleague would like to receive more information on our publications, please mail the completed form to the address below, and we will be happy to send you our latest catalog.

Add Your Name To Our Mailing List

Name:_____
(Please print)

Address:_____

Address:_____

City/State/Zip:_____

Telephone:(_____)_____

I am a:

_____ Psychologist   _____ Mental Health Counselor
_____ Psychiatrist   _____ Marriage and Family Therapist
_____ School Psychologist   _____ Not in Mental Health Field
_____ Clinical Social Worker   _____ Other:_____

Add A Colleague To Our Mailing List

Name:_____
(Please print)

Address:_____

Address:_____

City/State/Zip:_____

Telephone:(_____)_____

I am a:

_____ Psychologist   _____ Mental Health Counselor
_____ Psychiatrist   _____ Marriage and Family Therapist
_____ School Psychologist   _____ Not in Mental Health Field
_____ Clinical Social Worker   _____ Other:_____

Mail To: Professional Resource Press
P.O. Box 15560
Sarasota, FL 34277-1560